ENGLISH LANGUAGE

FOR BEGINNERS™

D0293897

BY MICHELLE LOWE and BEN GRAHAM

Writers and Readers Publishing, Inc.
P.O. Box 461, Village Station
New York, NY 10014

Writers and Readers Limited
35 Britannia Row
London N1 8QH
Tel: 0171 226 3377
Fax: 0171 359 1454
e-mail: begin@writersandreaders.com

2A225-68

A Writers and Readers Documentary Comic Book
Copyright © 1998
ISBN # 0-86316-263-0 Trade
1 2 3 4 5 6 7 8 9 0

420

Printed in Finland by WSOY

Beginners Documentary Comic Books are published by Writers and Readers Publishing, Inc. Its trademark, consisting of the words "For Beginners, Writers and Readers Documentary Comic Books" and the Writers and Readers logo, is registered in the U. S. Patent and Trademark Office and in other countries.

publishing FOR BEGINNERS™ books continuously since 1975

1975:Cuba • 1976: Marx • 1977: Lenin • 1978: Nuclear Power • 1979: Einstein • Freud • 1980: Mao • Trotsky • 1981: Capitalism • 1982: Darwin • Economics • French Revolution • Marx's Kapital • Food • Ecology • 1983: DNA • Ireland • 1984: London • Peace • Medicine • Orwell • Reagan • Nicaragua • Black History • 1985: Mark Diary • 1986: Zen • Psychiatry • Reich • Socialism • Computers • Brecht • Elvis • 1988: Architecture • Sex • JFK • Virginia Woolf • 1990: Nietzsche • Plato • Malcolm X • Judaism • 1991: WWII • Erotica • African History • 1992: Philosophy • • Rainforests • Miles Davis • Islam • Pan Africanism • 1993: Black Women • Arabs and Israel • 1994: Babies • Foucault • Heidegger • Hemingway • Classical Music • 1995: Jazz • Jewish Holocaust • Health Care • Domestic Violence • Sartre • United Nations • Black Holocaust • Black Panthers • Martial Arts • History of Clowns • 1996: Opera • Biology • Saussure • UNICEF • Kierkegaard • Addiction & Recovery • I Ching • Buddha • Derrida • Chomsky • McLuhan • Jung • 1997: Lacan • Shakespeare • Structuralism • Che • 1998: Fanon • Adler • Marilyn • Cinema • Postmodernism

Contents

Chapter One   - History   *1*

    THE ORIGINS OF LANGUAGE   *2*

    THE ORIGINS OF ENGLISH   *13*

    THE ORIGINS OF LINGUISTICS   *37*

Chapter Two - Child Language Acquisition   *42*

    DEVELOPMENTAL STAGES   *43*

    THE THEORIES   *66*

Chapter Three - Sex and Power   *85*

    SEX AND SPEECH   *86*

    BIAS AND LANGUAGE   *106*

    POWER AND LANGUAGE   *130*

Chapter Four - Variety and Change   *145*

    LANGUAGE VARIETIES   *146*

    LANGUAGE CHANGE   *169*

Index   *194*

Bibliography   *198*

Acknowledgments   *204*

DEDICATION

THANK YOU

THANK YOU

THANK YOU...

... GEORGINA VINCE AND SEAN DECAMP OF STRODE COLLEGE. THANKS ARE ALSO DUE TO MATT, MEG, TIM AND THE REST OF BOTH OUR FAMILIES AS WELL AS THE VERY KIND PROFESSOR DAVID CRYSTAL

chapter one:

HISTORY

Part 1

THE ORIGINS ⓕ LANGUAGE pg.2

✎ When did humans first use language?

✎ How did language develop?

✎ What was the first language?

✎ Where did it come from?

Part 2

THE ORIGINS ⓕ ENGLISH pg.13

✎ Where did English come from?

✎ How has English changed over time?

Part 3

THE ORIGINS ⓕ LINGUISTICS pg.37

✎ Who were the first linguists
and what did they discover?

PART ONE

THE ORIGINS OF LANGUAGE

None of these questions can be answered with any certainty; there just isn't enough evidence to know for sure. But, I suppose, we should at least try...

FIRST: WHEN?

Before we tackle this, we've got to ask what language actually *is.* Almost all animals communicate – some, like birds, have highly complex communication systems that seem as unpredictable as ours.

So, what is it that makes human communication 'language'?

THE ANSWER, IN SHORT, IS GRAMMAR. ALL ANIMAL COMMUNICATION SYSTEMS SEEM TO FIT INTO 1 OF 3 BASIC DESIGNS...

1. A FINITE VOCABULARY OF CALLS VERVET MONKEYS HAVE ONE CALL TO WARN OF LARGE GROUND PREDATORS, ONE FOR AIRBORNE PREDATORS, ONE FOR SNAKES, ETC.

2. A CONTINUOUS REPETITIVE SIGNAL THAT VARIES IN INTENSITY ACCORDING TO THE IMPORTANCE OF THE MESSAGE THE MORE ENERGETIC THE BEES' DANCE, THE MORE VALUABLE THE FOOD SOURCE THEY HAVE DISCOVERED

3. A REPEATED THEME WITH RANDOM VARIATIONS A BIRD REPEATS A SONG WITH A NEW TWIST EACH TIME

(WILSON 1972, GOULD AND MARLER 1987)

Though complex, these systems have built-in limitations that restrict their users to a finite number of expressions. For example, a Vervet monkey can't distinguish between a panther and a leopard and a bee can't communicate anything beyond the subject matter of nectar.

And instead, humans have GRAMMAR?

Yes – but not the kind they teach in school. We are talking about <u>a set of internal rules for understanding and using language</u>, sometimes called 'mental grammar'. This complicated framework of rules allows us to create an infinite number of meanings. There is no limit to the number of words or sentences we can use and create. Grammar is adaptable to any concept that we wish to communicate.

Human language also comes from a different part of the brain to that of other animals. For example, the calls of primates are controlled by structures in the stem of the brain which are closely linked with emotion.

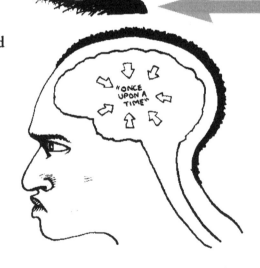

Human speech, however, is controlled mainly by areas in the upper left hemisphere of the brain which also process sensory perception, logical reasoning and perception of time (Pinker 1994 p.306).

Human vocalisations that *are* controlled by the same brain areas as the primates are things like crying, laughing and shouting with pain or fright. The difference is clear.
(Pinker 1994 p.334).

So back to the question in hand:

WHEN did humans start using a 'language' with this magical 'grammar' stuff anyway?

Well, language obviously didn't just appear on a specific date or with the birth of a particular human being, it **evolved** over something like **5 to 7 million years** (Pinker 1994 p.345). Over this time, there were many species of humans, all with varying linguistic abilities according to how they were built. So, we have to bear in mind that the **vocal abilities** of some may not have been as developed as their **language**: the distinction between **language** and **speech** is important.

HERE'S A ROUGH HISTORY:

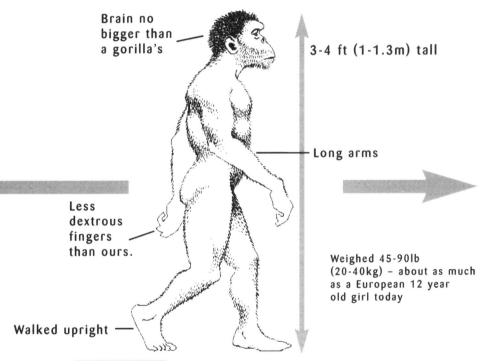

Brain no bigger than a gorilla's

3-4 ft (1-1.3m) tall

Long arms

Less dextrous fingers than ours.

Weighed 45-90lb (20-40kg) – about as much as a European 12 year old girl today

Walked upright

About 4 million B.C. the earth was roamed by a species of human called AUSTRALOPITHECUS AFRICANUS who, according to most authorities, didn't use language any more than primates do. Their vocal control was probably better than that of modern primates. It is quite possible, however, that these humans had a 'proto-language' – a language that was partially developed with fewer complexities and less consistent rules.

One way of assessing whether a species might have had language is to examine any artifacts that they leave behind, because the more sophisticated the relics, the more complex we can assume their creators minds to have been. We haven't found any evidence of 'civilised artifacts' from this period, and so most people are sceptical about the language abilities of Australopithecus.

Steven Pinker disputes this however. He points out that there are many modern hunter-gatherer peoples with sophisticated language and technology, whose tools and weapons aren't stone and would rot away to nothing in a short time. It is quite possible that Australopithecus had both tools and language; we just can't find any evidence to prove it
(Pinker 1994 p.352).

Bigger Brain (but still only 1/2 the size of ours)

Smaller face and jaw

About 4-5 ft tall (1.2-1.5m)

Arms shorter than Australopithecus's

Hands more like ours with strong but sensitive grip

Hip bones suited to bidepal walking and giving birth to babies with large heads

Weighed 100lb (50Kg)

By 2.5-2 Million BCE the species known as **HOMO HABILIS** was leaving collections of stone tools in places that could have been early slaughter-houses, homes or other community centres. This makes a fairly strong case for the existence of **language** by this time.

By **200,000 BCE** some **Hominids** (early humans) had developed vocal equipment similar to ours, but they still may not have had nervous systems efficient enough to control it with the accuracy needed for sophisticated **spoken language**.

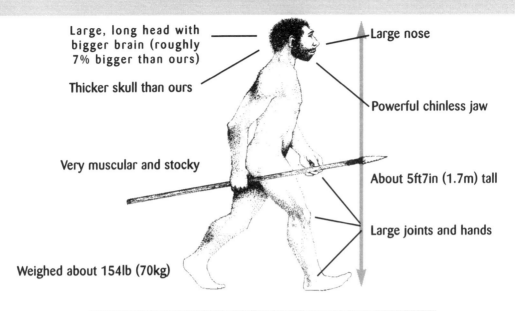

Large, long head with bigger brain (roughly 7% bigger than ours)

Thicker skull than ours

Very muscular and stocky

Weighed about 154lb (70kg)

Large nose

Powerful chinless jaw

About 5ft7in (1.7m) tall

Large joints and hands

c.70,000-35,000 BCE A more famous species, the **NEANDERTHALS**, inhabited most of Europe, the Near East and Northern Africa. They definitely had a sophisticated life-style involving things like wearing clothes, making and using tools, burying their dead and even performing religious rituals – **which all suggests that they used language.**

Their skeletons show that their vocal tracts probably weren't developed enough to handle sophisticated **speech,** so that Neanderthal speech (if it existed) would have had a limited range of vowel sounds. That's not to say it was hindered by this though; fewer vowels don't necessarily mean a less expressive language.

And then c. **30,000 BCE BANG!** For some unknown reason, the Neanderthals suddenly disappeared without trace. No explanation has yet been found for this, perhaps they died out, perhaps they left in a spaceship – no one knows.

Their absence, however, allowed another species of human – **HOMO SAPIENS** – to become dominant. These people, also known as the **CRO-MAGNON,** were basically us – the same in biology and in brain. They had been spreading across the globe for 70,000 years and had co-existed with the Neanderthals for 30,000 years, without interbreeding.

The **Cro-magnons** quickly reached a higher level of cultural and intellectual development. They made cave paintings (such as those at Lascaux in France and Altimara in Spain), they designed a wide range of high quality tools and weapons (lighter and more effective than those of the Neanderthals) and they had a sophisticated knowledge of fire and its uses. It seems that they also had better hunting methods than their forebears (hunting particular animals according to season, and hunting in teams co-operatively).

They definitely had language similar, if not identical, in complexity to our own. As for **speech**, they shared an important physical characteristic with modern man, which made their speech more flexible than their predecessors - all will be revealed soon.

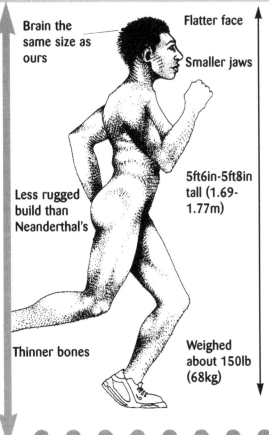

Brain the same size as ours

Flatter face

Smaller jaws

Less rugged build than Neanderthal's

5ft6in-5ft8in tall (1.69-1.77m)

Thinner bones

Weighed about 150lb (68kg)

So, to sum up: language evolved over a hugely long time in conjunction with the evolution of the human race. It is quite possible that humans as early as Australopithecus (4 million years ago) had traces of language and it is certain that, by the time of the Neanderthals, it was well established.

Language may not have become anything familiar until as late as 100,000 or even 50,000 BCE with the rise of the Cro-magnons, but it has certainly been around in various forms for much longer than that... phew!

NEXT, HOW?

The development of human **language** was probably down to NATURAL SELECTION (discovered by the ever-so-famous Charles Darwin).

I THINK YOU'D BETTER EXPLAIN.

● Well, millions of years ago, a human being was born who was slightly different from her parents. The difference was that there was a **mutation** (a random genetic change) which had altered the wiring in her brain a little.

● This alteration turned out, quite by chance, to give the human (and her brothers and sisters who may also have had the mutation) a slightly better ability to communicate. Perhaps it helped them to understand the instinctive calls of their fellows quicker or to use the calls and signals more effectively themselves.

● Because humans relied on co-operation and community bonds for their survival, those who had this mutation rose to prosperity, gaining status and attracting lots of strong, intelligent mates.

● They bred and, because genetic mutations are hereditary, they passed their ability on to their children. The next generation was also successful, spreading the mutation further.

● Over time, those who didn't have the mutation gradually died out (they gained fewer and weaker mates because of their less refined communication abilities) – NATURAL SELECTION.

● Once the mutation had gripped the population, those with the most pronounced version of it became the most successful and passed on their strength. By this process, the mutation grew and evolved over the millennia into an entirely new part of the brain, providing more and better powers of communication with each new generation.

● As the human race evolved, so too did its language.

So, what was this about the Cro-magnons having some physical difference?

SPEECH: THE ESSENTIAL DIFFERENCE

There was an all-important difference between the Cro-magnon people and their predecessors. Basically, their larynx (the cavity containing the vocal cords) was lower down in their throats. This meant two things:

1. When they swallowed, their food had to pass over their larynx on its way to the gullet, and consequently, unlike any other animal, they risked accidentally inhaling and choking on it.

2. They had longer, more flexible pharyngeal cavities, meaning they could produce a greater range of sounds and have better control over them – they could speak far more flexibly and expressively than their predecessors.

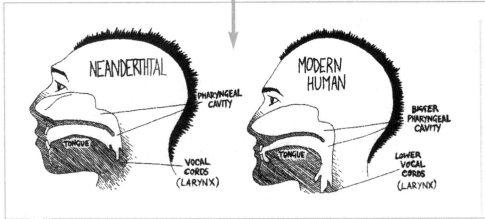

NEANDERTHTAL

PHARYNGEAL CAVITY

TONGUE

VOCAL CORDS (LARYNX)

MODERN HUMAN

BIGGER PHARYNGEAL CAVITY

TONGUE

LOWER VOCAL CORDS (LARYNX)

So, people could speak long before HOMO SAPIENS came along. But speech did get a real boost at that point because our larynx dropped a few centimetres.

WHAT? AND WHERE?

These two questions are linked by their answers. There are two main theories about the origins of the world's languages:

1. They developed across the globe from a number of separate languages, which arose at roughly the same time in different places. (POLYGENESIS)

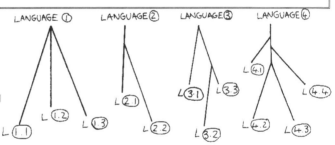

The evidence in support of this idea is fairly obvious: just look at the differences between the languages of the world. For instance, compare Japanese with French, or with any other language for that matter. Apart from sharing some of its vocabulary and writing system with Chinese, Japanese seems to have nothing in common with any other language. If this is the case, Japanese must have developed from a different root to other languages.

What's more, many languages exist in places that have been geographically cut off from the rest of the world e.g. the *Dravidian languages* of Southern India and Sri Lanka and the *Luorawetlan languages* of Eastern Siberia. It seems that these languages must have developed independently of the 20,000 main global language families (Bryson 1990 p.14).

> Or, 2. They all come from a single mother language that originated in one place and split into different languages as its speakers migrated away from each other across the planet. (MONOGENESIS)

Despite the arguments above, there is support for this idea. It is backed up by the existence of connections between languages, or **COMMON COGNATES** – words of similar meaning that are spelled in similar ways in more than one language, e.g.

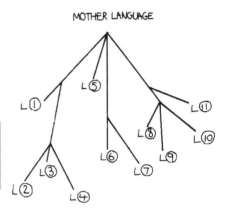

FRENCH	-	'tu'
ENGLISH	-	'thou'
HITTITE	-	'tuk'

Also, there are a growing number of languages that were, like Japanese, thought to be unique, but have now been found to have connections with the most obscure partners.

For instance, the native American language families *Eskimo-Aleut, Amerind* and *Na-Dene* were long thought to be unrelated to anything else including each other. **However,** *Na-Dene* (spoken in North-West USA and Canada) has been found to have links with Basque, which is an ancient language (possibly even Neolithic) spoken by 600,000 people in Spain and 100,000 in France around the Bay of Biscay. *Eskimo-Aleut* has been found to have connections with Finnish (Bryson 1990 pp.14 and 15).

> Yes, but surely 2 completely different languages could swap words if their speakers met?

That's true, it's possible that some of those similarities could be explained by **CONVERGENCE** – totally separate languages passing on minor features, like vocabulary or even mixing and bonding to form new languages when speakers encounter each other through migration, cohabitation, war or any other form of contact. Unfortunately, this doesn't get us any closer to knowing **WHAT** the first language was or **WHERE** it was spoken, in fact, we've just exposed doubt about whether there was a 'first' language.

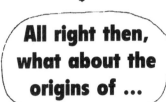

PART TWO

All right then, what about the origins of ...

ENGLISH?

Well, before we go into that we'd better quickly look at how linguists study the origins of a language...

There are various methods of classifying languages but the most widely used is the 'GENETIC' or 'GENEALOGICAL' method.

GENETIC CLASSIFICATION is the process linguists use to group languages into families by finding similarities between them (i.e. **common cognates**). Once this is done, they can be traced back to hypothetical parent languages.

Using this method (combined with studying whatever written remains are available – generally not many), linguists have managed to reconstruct the 'family trees' of most of the world's modern languages.

They've deduced that English belongs to the group of languages known as the **GERMANIC** family, which in turn belongs to the wider family of **INDO-EUROPEAN** languages which, they think, developed out of a parent language around 3000-4000 years ago. This hypothetical parent language has been named...

 PROTO-INDO-EUROPEAN

It is extremely difficult to tell where the Proto-Indo-Europeans came from because they left no written records. However, scholars have done some very clever guesswork.

LINGUISTIC GUESSWORK: This comes from looking at similarities in the vocabulary of its daughter languages. For example, there are no common words for *palm tree* or *vine* so they probably didn't come from the Mediterranean region. There are none for *sea* either, so they probably came from inland. There are similar words for *snow* and *cold* in all the Indo European languages, so they couldn't have come from a tropical climate.

This type of deduction suggests that the speakers of Proto-Indo-European came from somewhere between **inland Northern Europe and Southern Russia.**

ARCHEOLOGICAL GUESSWORK: Archaeologists have linked Proto-Indo-European to a race of semi-nomadic people living in **Southern Russia** in around 4000 BCE. Between 3500 and 2000 BCE this race, known as the **KURGANS**, spread across Europe taking their language with them.

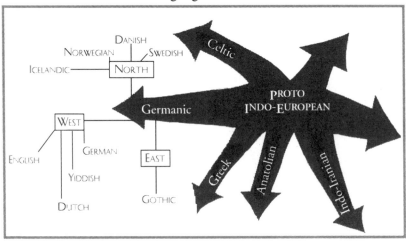

By 2000-1000 BCE Proto-Indo-European began to split up as its speakers moved apart. It split into the languages that make up the Indo-European family. The first written evidence of **Greek, Anatolian** and **Indo-Iranian** (all **Indo-European languages**) dates from around this time.

Much later (sometime before 10 BCE), there was a language on a western branch of the Indo-European family tree known as **PRIMITIVE GERMANIC** which, over the next thousand years, gradually developed into a number of new languages including **German, Dutch, Danish, Swedish, Icelandic** and **English.**

THE ARRIVAL OF ENGLISH IN ENGLAND

It wasn't until the **5th century CE** that the people who gave England its name and its language arrived on the island. For about a thousand years, the British Isles had been inhabited by the **Celts** – a race of people descended from the Kurgans, who spoke the linguistic ancestor of modern Cymric (Welsh) and the Gaelic of the Scots and Irish. For nearly half as long again they were part of the Roman Empire and the populace spoke a mixture of **Greek, Latin** and **Celtic.** Then in **410 CE**, the Romans departed to defend their empire in Europe, leaving the British tribes defenceless against any who should decide to come and visit.

In about 450 CE, four groups of people from Holland, Denmark and Germany – the ANGLES, the JUTES, the FRISIANS and the SAXONS – began a gradual settlement of Britain, a sort of long, drawn-out invasion.

They eventually established seven kingdoms covering the whole island except Scotland, Wales and Cornwall, which remained Celtic strongholds. Despite the fact that the Saxons were the dominant group, the new nation gradually became known as ENGLAND and its language as ENGLISH after the Angles.

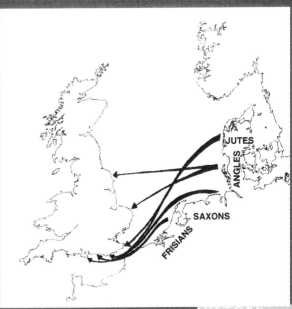

The history of English
has been divided into
four rough stages:

1. 'OLD ENGLISH' – from the **Anglo-Saxons up to around 1150**,

2. 'MIDDLE ENGLISH' – **1150** to about **1475-1500**,

3. 'EARLY MODERN' – **up to about 1700** and

4. 'MODERN ENGLISH' – bringing us up to the **present day.**

These dates are, of course, approximate since there is no way of pinning down actual turning points between stages. The language is in a constant state of flux; these divisions just mark major changes and make it easier to discuss.

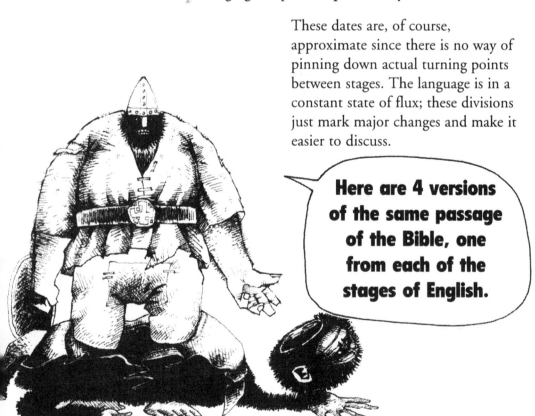

Here are 4 versions
of the same passage
of the Bible, one
from each of the
stages of English.

OLD ENGLISH

Ne mæg nān man twām hlāfordum þēowian, oððe hē sōþlice ānne hataþ, and ōðerne lufaþ; oððe hē biþ ānum gehȳrsum, and ōðrum ungehȳrsum. Ne māgon gē Gode þēowian and woruldwelan. Forðām ic secge ēow, ðæt gë ne sīn ymbhȳdige ēowre sāwle, hwæt gē eton; ne ēowrum līchaman, mid hwām gē sȳn ymbscrȳdde. Hū nys sēo sāwl sēlre ðonne mete, and ēower līchāma betera ðonne ðæt rēaf? Behealdaþ heofonan

MIDDLE ENGLISH

No man may serue to two lordis, forsothe ethir he shal haat the toon, and loue the tother; other he shal susteyn the toon, and dispise the tothir. ȝe mown nat serue to God and richessis. Therfore Y say to ȝou, that ȝe ben nat besie to ȝoure lijf, what ȝe shulen ete; othir to ȝoure body, with what ȝe shuln be clothid. Wher ȝoure lijf is nat more than mete, and the body more than clothe? Beholde ȝe the fleȝinge foulis of the eir,

EARLY MODERN ENGLISH

No man can serue two masters: for either he will hate the one and loue the other, or else hee will holde to the one, and despise the other. Ye cannot serue God and Mammon. Therfore I say vnto you, Take no thought for your life, what yee shall eate, or what ye shall drinke, nor yet for your body, what yee shall put on: Is not the life more then meate? and the body then raiment? Behold the foules of the aire: for they sow not,

MODERN ENGLISH

No servant can be slave to two masters; for either he will hate the first and love the second, or he will be devoted to the first and think nothing of the second. You cannot serve God and Money. Therefore I bid you put away anxious thoughts about food and drink to keep you alive, and clothes to cover your body. Surely life is more than food, the body more than clothes.

OLD ENGLISH
c. 450 - 1150

Even though we know the Anglo-Saxons had an alphabet, it seems that the invaders were virtually illiterate and had little interest in recording any area of life. Writings from the period are so scarce, in fact, that there is a complete gap in history up until the beginning of the **7th century** when **St. Augustine**, a Roman catholic missionary and his band of 40 monks were sent in **597 AD** to reintroduce Christianity to the British Isles. St. Augustine was very successful, and in no time at all, Christianity had spread across the country.

With Christianity came literacy. Soon people were writing all sorts of things down all over the place and within about 100 years Britain became a centre of learning in Europe, with religious manuscripts being brought in from Rome and the Bible being copied and translated from Latin into the native dialects across the country.

GENERAL CERTIFICATE OF SAXON EDUCATION.

So what happened to the Celts then?

CELTIC INFLUENCE ON OLD ENGLISH
The Celts were so forcibly pushed to the extremes of the island that their language made very little impact on that of the invaders. Quite a few English place names are of Celtic origin, (e.g. **'London'**, **'Dover'**, **'Avon'** and **'Thames'**) but hardly any other Celtic words remain in common use.

LATIN INFLUENCE ON OLD ENGLISH

The Roman Empire had an early influence on the Anglo-Saxons – again there are place names of Latin origin (e.g. the 'chester' part of names such as **Dorchester** and **Manchester**). The Anglo-Saxons also took a great many words from the Romans before they came to England: they lived on the edge of the Roman Empire and borrowed words for common, everyday objects and concepts like '*street*', '*wine*', '*inch*', '*mile*', '*pit*', '*table*' and '*chest*'.

Later, when St. Augustine brought God and literacy to England, the language gained even more from Latin – '**monk**', '**noon**' and '**abbot**' being among the words gained. Latin continued to influence English throughout the Middle Ages, but more of that later.

OLD ENGLISH GRAMMAR

Old English was what is known as an **INFLECTED** language. That is to say that, like Latin, German and Russian, it used various endings for words – **INFLECTIONS** – to express relationships between them. For example, here are the various ways of constructing a sentence in Old English around the word 'stone':

	CASE	SINGULAR	PLURAL
O L D E N G L I S H	**NOMINATIVE**	*stan* - subject 'this stone is heavy'	*stanas* - subject 'these stones are heavy'
	ACCUSATIVE	*stan* - object 'I picked up a stone'	*stanas* - object 'I picked up some stones'
	GENITIVE	*stanes* - possessive 'the stone's colour was beautiful'	*stana* - possessive 'the stones' colours were beautiful'
	DATIVE	*stane* 'with, by, to, for, from (etc.) a stone'	*stanum* 'with, by, to, from, for (etc.) stones'

(Wakelyn 1980 pp.21-2)

You can see these different cases being used in the earliest of the Bible extracts e.g. '*æfterm six dagum*' ('after six days') where the plural noun '*dagum*' is in the dative case.

By the end of the 8th century, Christianity had settled the four corners of England, literacy was widely spread and the country was as civilised as it had been in Roman times. And then, wouldn't you just **know** it...

MORE HAIRY INVADERS!!!!

For who-knows-what reason, the Germanic tribespeople decided to invade **again**. This time it was the **VIKINGS**, who were even more savage and brutal than the previous attackers. Beginning in **793**, there were seemingly random smash 'n' grab raids on the East Coast which then ended as suddenly as they had begun.

Then in **850 CE**, 350 Viking ships sailed up the river Thames, setting off territorial battles that lasted for decades. Fighting continued right up to the beginning of the **11th century** when, finally, **in 1013** a Dane called Swein Forkbeard became king of all England.

THE EFFECT OF OLD NORSE

Old Norse (the Vikings' language) had many similarities with Old English, so the natives and the invaders could probably just about understand each other when they first met. Old Norse merged easily and rapidly with Old English virtually all over Britain, except in really isolated places like the Shetland Isles, where the division remained intact for centuries.

Old Norse did have an effect on English though, right?!

1. It brought about a general clarification and strengthening of the language, **filling gaps in the vocabulary** and encouraging the process of **dropping redundant grammatical** features (e.g. inflected endings).

2. English gained a huge number of words from the Old Norse dialects, including *scythe, rubbish, ladder, freckle, leg, skull, meek, rotten, churn, clasp, crawl, law, dazzle, scream, trust, lift, take, husband, sky, window* and *flick*. It also gained many new place names especially in the north of England where over 1400 place names are of Norse origin (Bryson 1990 p.45).

3. English took on elements of Norse grammar, like the prepositions *up, down, in, out, off, from, take, to,* and the pronouns *they, them and their,* which improved the clarity of the language no end. Because, before the change, *he* for example could mean either *he* or *they*, depending on the context.

English was really starting to take shape by this time, but it wasn't out of the woods yet...there was one more major shake-up to come...

ANOTHER INVASION !!!

These invaders came from France but they were virtually the same people as the last lot. The Normans were descendants of Vikings who had settled in Northern France at roughly the same time as those who had arrived in England. Unlike the settlers in Britain, however, these Norsemen almost totally abandoned their native language and culture, becoming French in every way.

In **1066**, when William the Conqueror came across the Channel and earned his name, he brought with him not standard, Parisian French, but **a rural French dialect** which quickly took root in England. In doing so it moved even further from the 'standard' French spoken in Paris (to the extent that it earned the name **'Anglo-Norman'** from historians). The Normans took over all positions of authority – establishing a wholly French aristocracy, government and court.

It was the Norman invasion that marked the beginning of the transition from Old English to...

MIDDLE ENGLISH
1150 - C.1500

The Old English period is usually said to have finished about a hundred years after the arrival of the Normans because it took until about **1150** for Anglo-Norman to become the standard literary language as well as the language of court and politics.

THE EFFECT ⓕ ANGLO NORMAN

Anglo-Norman had a dramatic impact on the language even though the common people continued speaking Old English. (They didn't come into contact much with the lives of the Anglo-Norman-speaking ruling classes).

MIDDLE ENGLISH SPELLING

When the Normans arrived, English spelling was in a peculiar state because its sound system had undergone dramatic changes since Anglo-Saxon times, but the spellings had barely changed.

The French scribes updated the spelling of many English sounds. For instance, instead of using the letter c to represent the sounds in '**king**', '**cow**', and '**chime**'(as it had been done in Old English), they employed the letters we use today.

In addition to this, modern letters gradually replaced old ones like **æ**, **ß** and **Ø**.

MIDDLE ENGLISH VOCABULARY

English gained around **10,000 new words,** three quarters of which are still in common usage (Bryson 1990 p.47).
Because it was the upper classes who spoke French, most of this vocabulary referred to aspects of high society and stays with us as formal/literary language.

For Example:

WORDS OF ANGLO-SAXON ORIGIN	WORDS OF ANGLO-NORMAN ORIGIN
builder	mason
shoemaker	tailor
clothes	fashion
sheep	mutton
cow	beef
pig	bacon/pork
underwear	lingerie
meet	encounter
worker	employee
drunk	intoxicated
house	residence
talk	converse

Added to this, where English and French met, lots of new grammatical constructions were possible. For example:
unreasonable (Old English prefix *un-* + Old French *raisonable*)
companionship (Old French *compagne* + Old English *-scipe*)
bearable (Old English *beran* + Old French *-able*)

MIDDLE ENGLISH GRAMMER

The Norman Conquest encouraged the demise of inflected endings. For example, in Middle English, all the endings for the word *stone* (see pg. 19) had been replaced by the system that we use today. There were now two possibilities: *stoon* (singular) or *stoones* (plural).

Another reason for this development was the fact that in English, words are generally stressed on the first syllable – <u>ta</u>ble, <u>break</u>fast, <u>cab</u>bage. So, the unstressed endings of words become less and less important and vowels gradually degrade into an indeterminate sound (as in the last vowel of lett<u>er</u> and mutt<u>on</u>). Because of this, all the inflectional endings in Old English gradually lost their emphasis and definition, then eventually faded out of use altogether (Wakelyn 1980 p.25).

If you compare the first two Bible extracts, (see pg. 17) you can easily see the difference for yourself.

ENGLISH AS STANDARD

In the **13th** and **14th** centuries, English began to re-emerge as an accepted standard language (rather than being just for the peasants). There were several reasons for this:

1. In **1204**, the Anglo-Norman ruler, King John, lost Normandy to France. This served to detach the Norman-English ruling classes further from their original homeland. They began to think of themselves as more English than French.

2. This feeling was intensified by intermarrying between the Normans and English, which was common by this time.

Between **1348** and **1350**, the country was swept by the Black Death, which killed over 30% of the population. This drastically reduced the workforce throughout England, so surviving members of the working classes suddenly became far more important and valuable (there were less of them to go round). As the status of the common people rose, so too did that of their language – English.

SO, ☛1. Anglo-Norman gradually became less fashionable and less commonplace while English gradually regained status. By **1332**, Parliament had become worried and decreed that,

'**All Lords, Barons, Knights and honest men of good towns should exercise care and diligence to teach their children the French language...**'
(Baugh and Cable 1978)

☛2. By the end of the **14th** century, the situation had become so serious that Oxford University had decreed that all its students must use both French and English '*lest the French language be entirely disused*'.

☛3. In October **1362**, Parliament was opened in English for the first time and it was ruled that all court proceedings be conducted in English.

☛4. Towards the end of the **14th** century important literary works were published in English. During the last decades of the **14th** century (c. **1370** onwards), **Geoffrey Chaucer** wrote a number of famous poems, the most well known of which are *The Canterbury Tales*. Although he also spoke French and Italian and used a great deal of vocabulary from these languages, it was English that he chose to produce his works in and this further raised its status.

By the end of the 15th century, English was once again the first language of the English.

STANDARD ENGLISH

When English resurfaced as the standard, it did so in the form of four very different main dialects: **Northern, East Midland, West Midland** and **Southern** and the smaller sub-dialect, **Kentish.** Although there is no way of telling what the spoken dialects may have sounded like or how distant they were from each other, it is certain that in writing, they were far removed from one another.

Compare the following,

Whan that Aprille with his shoures sote
The droghte of Marche hath perced to the rote,
And bathed every veyne in swich licour,
Of which vertu engendred is the flour,

'And vorlet ous oure yeldinge, ase and we vorlotep oure yelderes, and ne ous led na t, in-to vondinge, ac vri ous vram queade.'

As you can see, Chaucer's passage is far easier to understand than the Lord's Prayer extract. This is because the London and East Midland dialect he used later became the standard while the other dialects, including Kentish, all but died out.

WHY DID EAST MIDLAND BECOME THE STANDARD?

1.GEOGRAPHY: It was spoken in the region between the two extremes of Northern and Southern and, because it shared features from both, it represented a kind of compromise between them.

2. ECONOMIC INFLUENCE: The East Midland region had the largest and most affluent population, and was the biggest and agriculturally richest of the four regions.

3. ACADEMIC INFLUENCE: By the 14th century, the universities of Oxford and Cambridge were gaining increasing intellectual influence as monasteries were losing their monopoly over literacy and education.

4. THE CAPITAL: London was the commercial, political, legal and social capital of the country and thus was highly influential in all of these areas. By the 15th century, the dialect spoken in London had shifted from Southern to East Midland (perhaps because most of the commercial traffic came from the East Midland region). As the influence of London spread, so too did its dialect.

EARLY MDERN ENGLISH

(ALSO KNOWN AS THE RENAISSANCE
& SOMETIMES DATED c.1500 - 1650)

This period is not marked by any major historical events like battles, diseases or invasions, but by the development of some general social factors:

PRINTING

In 1476, William Caxton set up **England's first printing press** in Westminster, London. He had learned the technique in Europe, where thousands of books had already been published.

Printing spread fast and, by the end of the Early Modern period, over 20,000 titles had been printed in England, from huge tomes to tiny pamphlets, and manuscript books (hand copied) were all but obsolete.

EDUCATION

As books became more available, literacy increased. By the end of the Early Modern period, as much as half the population of London could at least read (Baugh and Cable 1978, p.200). And in the 17th and 18th centuries, the new middle class of traders and merchants had the time and means to educate themselves and their children. The number of schools grew and grew, and novels and newspapers became ever more popular.

COMMUNICATION

Advances in global travel and trade brought foreign
thinking, techniques and inventions to England and with
them came new vocabulary. In fact, between 1530 and
1660 English underwent the fastest lexical growth in its
history (Crystal 1995 p.72). First, the new words came
mainly from the continent...

FROM LATIN AND GREEK

Greek

adapt, appropriate, atmosphere,
benefit, catastrophe, chaos, crisis,
disrespect, emancipation, exaggerate,
exist, explain, fact, immaturity,
impersonal, monopoly, obstruction,
pathetic, relevant, scheme, skeleton,
temperature, vacuum, virus. . .

FROM OR VIA SPANISH AND PORTUGUESE

Spaniard

alligator, apricot, banana,
cannibal, guitar, hammock,
mosquito, negro, potato,
tobacco. . .

Spaniard

FROM OR VIA ITALIAN

An Italian Dancer

balcony, ballot,
concerto, design,
fuse, giraffe,
lottery, opera,
rocket, solo,
sonata, violin,
volcano. . .

FROM OR VIA FRENCH

alloy, anatomy,
battery, chocolate,
detail, duel,
entrance, explore,
invite, muscle,
passport,
probability, shock,
ticket, tomato,
vase. . .

Monsieur from Paris

(AND THIS IS A **VERY** SMALL SELECTION)

Later, with world-wide exploration, words began coming in **from all over the place, e.g.,** *ketchup* and *bamboo* from Malay, *coffee, kiosk* and *yogurt* from Turkish, *curry* from Tamil and *racoon* from Algonquian.

On top of this, new words were being created out of what already existed in English by adding prefixes and suffixes: *disrobe, endear, nonsense, submarine, uncomfortable, considerable, gloomy, immaturity* and the list goes on (Crystal 1995 p.60).

SO WHAT EFFECT DID ALL THIS HAVE THEN?

● Language Standardisation On the one hand, the spread of printing and education helped to standardise spellings and word meanings (multiple copies of books were printed with identical spellings) and, as books were printed in London, this further helped the London dialect (East Midland) to become the written standard.

● Language Change On the other hand, the influx of foreign words and ideas was encouraging writers to be inventive with vocabulary and create new words (e.g. Thomas Elyot who used foreign and new words to 'augment' and 'enrich' the language).

● Controversy There were those that believed that;

'Our tung shold be written cleane and pure, vnmixt and vnmangeled with borrowing of other tunges'. (John Cheke 1557 Crystal 1995 p.61)

Supporters of this view wrote in a very conservative style, using old grammar and vocabulary and avoiding any new words or constructions. An example of this type of writing from the time is the King James Bible.

Others, like William Shakespeare (1564-1616), deliberately used as much outlandish and exciting new vocab as they could. A huge number of common phrases and terms in use today were actually introduced by Shakespeare, e.g. **'in the minds eye'**, **'a foregone conclusion'** and **'a tower of strength'**. He also popularised a huge number of new words, e.g. **'obscene'**, **'accommodation'**, **'laughable'** and **'assassination'**.

Academics argued bitterly over the subject of **'inkhorn'** terms, as they were called: **are foreign words a detriment to the language or valuable addition?** The debate goes on to this day.

MDERN ENGLISH

C.1700 - PRESENT DAY

The most important thing that developed during this period **is an interest in language itself.** By the 18th century, England was becoming the centre of a huge empire and London English was a global language. Social boundaries were more fluid than ever – people could now improve their social status through learning and education (a large part of which was learning to 'improve' their use of language).

SO, academics became more and more interested in looking at language from an intellectual viewpoint, gauging its importance to the colonies and its relevance to society.

DICTIONARIES

In **1604**, a schoolteacher named Robert Cawdrey published the *Table Alphabeticall*, which contained definitions for around *3000 'hard vsual English wordes'*. It was a great success and was followed by many more over the following years. Each new dictionary that was published boasted a bigger word count – mainly because, spared of tiresome copyright laws, the authors simply stole their predecessors' definitions and added more of their own. So by 1736, in the third edition of **Bailey's** *Universal Etymological English Dictionary* the count had reached around **60,000** words. However, word counts aren't everything...

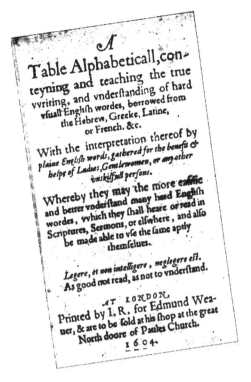

Johnson's Dictionary

It wasn't until **Dr Samuel Johnson's book** was published in 1755 that the language gained a truly comprehensive dictionary. Even though it had fewer definitions than Bailey's (only around 40,000), Johnson's was wider ranging and more practical. It had more common, everyday words and the definitions were more complete and informative. He used some 116,000 quotations from literary sources to support them. About half of these quotations came from **Dryden, Shakespeare, Milton, Addison, Bacon, Pope** and **the Bible,** what Johnson called,

The wells of English undefiled...

Johnson believed that

Tongues, like governments, have a natural tendency to degeneration...

and despite his claims that his intention was

Not form but register the language

his attitude, like that of his predecessors (who did things like dividing words into two categories: '**The choicest words**' and '**Vulgar words**' or marking disapproved of words with an 'obelisk'), was certainly PRESCRIPTIVE.

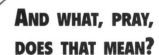

AND WHAT, PRAY, DOES THAT MEAN?

PRESCRIPTIVISM is the study of language with the intention of controlling it in some way – by dictating or **prescribing** how it ought to be used. This grew partly out of all the paranoia about the language being tainted and disrupted by all the changes that were happening in the Early Modern period.

HISTORY

THE PRESCRIPTIVE GRAMMARIANS

The Prescriptive Grammarians were a group of 18th-century academics who decided that they knew best and published guides on the use of *grammar...*

Although there had already been several works of this kind in the 17th century, the real craze started in the later half of the 18th. Over 200 'Grammars' were published between **1750** and **1800**. The most influential was *A Short Introduction to English Grammar* by Bishop **Robert Lowth**, which came out in **1762**. It contained 200 pages of fairly arbitrary, idiosyncratic rules on what grammatical forms should be avoided and which should be encouraged. He illustrated his rules with Shakespeare, Milton, Pope and others (Johnson's 'wells of English undefiled'). Lowth's grammatical rules became widely accepted and many still have influence today, e.g.

'Two negatives in English destroy one another, or are equivalent to an affirmative.'
This kind of judgement comes from the widely held idea that language should be logical – that any construction that isn't logical doesn't make sense.

'Never put a preposition at the end of a sentence.'
This rule, like many others, comes from the popular idea that English should follow the grammatical rules of Latin and Greek.

Why? What's so special about Latin?

LATIN was the historical language of the Bible, of the law courts, of the classics and of educated society. It was seen as pure and authoritative because, unlike English, it was an unchanging language that had strict rules for usage. (This was mainly because it was a dead language – no one actually used it for common communication and so it never changed or grew).

Some grammarians even went to the extent of writing their grammars *in* Latin. Books about *English* written *in Latin!* Can you believe it?!?

WE THE UNDERSIGNED WISH TO COMPLAIN THAT OUR LANGUAGE IS DAILY CORRUPTED AND ABUSED. WE DEMAND AN ACADEMY TO STEM THE DETERIORATION AND TO PROTECT OUR NOBLE LANGUAGE...

ACADEMIES

The **Académie Française** was set up by Cardinal Richelieu in 1635. Its main purpose was to
'Give definite rules to our language, and to render it pure, eloquent, and capable of treating the arts and sciences.' (Crystal 1987 p.4)
It published a dictionary in 1762 that regularised the spelling of about 5,000 words – around a quarter of the words in common use at the time.
In England in 1660, John Dryden complained that English was **'in a manner barbarous'** and proposed that English, too, should have an Academy. Over the next 2 centuries, lots of other academics including Daniel Defoe and Jonathan Swift agreed with him. They wanted to regulate language and to 'fix' it to prevent further change. But they never got their Academy and if they had, it is very unlikely that it would have lived up to their expectations. Throughout history, people have tried to halt language change; they are in fact still trying today, but language change is continuous and inevitable.

PART THREE

THE ORIGINS OF LINGUISTICS

Once established, linguistics moved through the following phases:

HISTORICAL Linguistics (19th century)
DESCRIPTIVE Linguistics (early 20th century) and
GENERATIVE Linguistics (1950s onwards)

HISTORICAL LINGUISTICS

1786 is often named as the year that linguistics was born, since this was the year in which **Sir William Jones** stated that Sanskrit (the ancient Indian language), Germanic, Latin, Celtic and Greek all came from the same source language. (He wasn't the first to say so, but history has given him the credit.) Over the next century, what with Darwin publishing his theory of evolution, the study of the evolution of languages became all the rage. All the research discussed earlier about the reconstruction of Proto-Indo-European and the development of Genetic Classification came out of Jones's discovery.

Another important discovery came in the 1870s, when a group of German linguists – the 'Neogrammarians' – claimed that **'sound laws have no exceptions'**. What they meant by this was that if a sound change occurs in any word of a dialect, then all the other similar occurrences of that sound will also change. For example, in Old English the word *chin* was pronounced 'kin'. When the 'k' sound in this word changed to *ch*, it did so in all other words where it was at the beginning of the word before *e* or *i* – *chicken, child, chip, chest,* etc. (Jean Aitchison, *Linguistics*, 1978 p.33).

So, historical linguistics was mainly about searching for the origins of languages and comparing different languages and how they changed over time.

DESCRIPTIVE LINGUISTICS

IN EUROPE:

The Swiss linguist, **Ferdinand De Saussure** has been dubbed by many as **'the father of modern linguistics'**. After his death in 1913, a group of his students collected his lecture notes together and published them under the title *Course in General Linguistics* (**1916**). Many of his ideas opened up the way for Descriptive Linguistics. Here are two really important ones:

1. SYNCHRONIC V DIACHRONIC

Saussure advocated studying language in two ways:
SYNCHRONIC and **DIACHRONIC**

1. DIACHRONIC STUDY is what his predecessors did: it's the study of language(s) over time as they evolve. Looking at the progression from Old English to modern English is Diachronic study.

2. SYNCHRONIC STUDY is about looking at a language in its entirety at one point in time. Describing what Old English was like in the 14th century (and not how it became Middle English), or looking at how English is spoken today in London is Synchronic study.
This might seem an obvious distinction to make, but it needed to be made, and there were lots of linguists before Saussure who didn't make it.

Ferdinand de Saussure (1857-1913)

2. LANGUAGE AS A SYSTEM

Saussure emphasised the fact that **language works as a system:** he described language as being like a game of chess – all the pieces have individual values, but these values are meaningless unless the pieces interact with each other. The value of each piece depends upon its position in relation to all the others – a move by one piece affects the whole system. In language, the meaning of a word in a sentence depends upon its position in that sentence, e.g.

'I have <u>no</u> chickens.' '<u>No</u>, I have chickens'
The analogy also applies in far more complex ways to language as a whole – a change in one element of a language affects the whole language. An example of this is what the Neogrammarians talked about with reference to pronunciation, except that Saussure applied it to all areas of language including grammar, and offered an explanation for why it should be so.

IN AMERICA

IN AMERICA linguistics grew out of an offshoot of anthropology. Around the beginning of the 20th century, American anthropologists/linguists were attempting to record the fast dying Native American languages. Unfortunately, without any kind of guidelines for describing them, their research was often inconsistent and unreliable.

In 1933, Leonard Bloomfield published a book called *Language* in which he attempted to establish a set of consistent rules for the description of languages. Like Saussure, he emphasised the importance of objective description of language.

Bloomfield was extremely influential; in fact the following twenty years have been dubbed '**The Bloomfieldian Era**'. During this time, many linguists wrote descriptive grammars (mostly of previously unwritten languages). This involved recording samples of people speaking that language, then analysing and cataloguing the utterances collected.

Prescriptive grammars lay down rules about how people should speak; descriptive grammars describe how language is used. Descriptive grammars are still commonplace today.

> SO, BASICALLY 'DESCRIPTIVE LINGUISTICS' IS ABOUT LOOKING AT LANGUAGE OBJECTIVELY IN ORDER TO ANALYSE ITS STRUCTURE.

These descriptive grammarians developed solid, rigorous research procedures – methods that remain as the standard today. Unfortunately, those involved got so caught up in the tiniest of grammatical details that by the 1950s, linguistics had become rather narrow-minded and inward looking. In 1957, another revolutionary thinker changed all that.

GENERATIVE LINGUISTICS

Noam Chomsky (b. 1928) is probably the most influential linguist of this century. He was a tutor at Massachusetts Institute of Technology when he published *Syntactic Structures* (1957). This book said that the search for a language's grammar based on collected utterances was a waste of time – it was a virtually impossible task and was, as he saw it, missing the most important point of linguistics anyway.

Instead, he wanted to create a **generative grammar**:

'A device which generates all the grammatical sequences of a language and none of the ungrammatical ones'.

He argued that speakers of a language must have a system inside their brains that allows them to create and understand an infinite number of different utterances – **a mental grammar** (as described at the beginning of this chapter). Theoretically, it should be possible to construct **a universal grammar** that applies to all natural languages – the mental grammar that we are all born with that allows us to learn and use language (but more on this in the Child Language Acquisition chapter).

Today (partly thanks to Chomsky), linguistics is a growing discipline which encompasses many types of study: synchronic, diachronic, descriptive grammars, the search for language universals or a universal grammar, psycholinguistics (the study of language and the mind), sociolinguistics (the study of language and society) and lots more. Next, we're moving on to how children learn language, so look out for Chomsky.

chapter Two:

CHILD LANGUAGE ACQUISITION

Part 1

DEVELOPMENTAL STAGES pg. 43

- When do children learn to talk?
  A study of language from one word to 50,000.

Part 2

THE THEORIES pg. 66

- Just how do children learn to talk?
  Some thoughts and arguments from linguists
  past and present.
- How important are parents (or caretakers)
  and what they say to their kids?

PART ONE

DEVELOPMENTAL STAGES

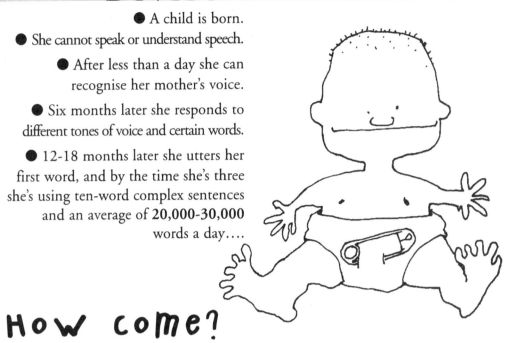

- A child is born.
- She cannot speak or understand speech.
- After less than a day she can recognise her mother's voice.
- Six months later she responds to different tones of voice and certain words.
- 12-18 months later she utters her first word, and by the time she's three she's using ten-word complex sentences and an average of **20,000-30,000** words a day....

How come?

There are many theories about how children manage this, but we'll get to those later. First, we'll look at the stages children's language goes through between an initial scream and adult coherence. These rough stages are followed by all 'normal children'* across the globe and have been dubbed **'DEVELOPMENTAL MILESTONES'**.

*i.e., those who receive adequate exposure to language and have no physiological impairments

The first of these major milestones is reached at about the age of **18 months** when the child speaks her first word, but even before this time children are busy learning how language works, (**PRAGMATICS**) and how it sounds, (**PHONOLOGY**).

For the first eight weeks of her life a child will make no more than what are called *reflexive noises*.

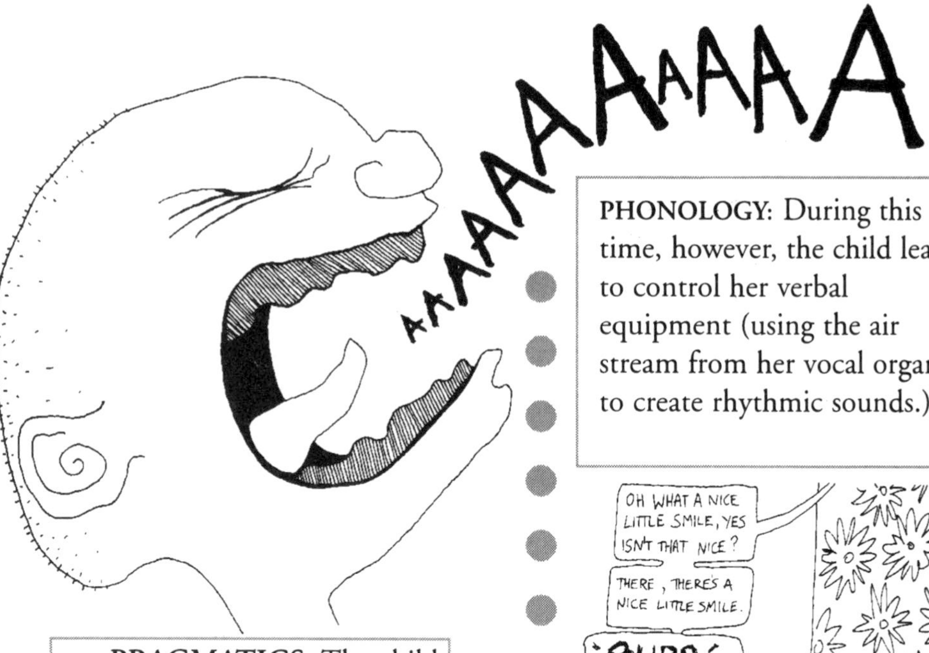

AAAAAAA AAA A

PHONOLOGY: During this time, however, the child learns to control her verbal equipment (using the air stream from her vocal organs to create rhythmic sounds.)

OH WHAT A NICE LITTLE SMILE, YES ISN'T THAT NICE?

THERE, THERE'S A NICE LITTLE SMILE.

:BURP:

WHAT A NICE LITTLE WIND AS WELL YES THAT'S BETTER ISN'T IT?

UH

THERE'S A NICE NOISE...

PRAGMATICS: The child discovers that different screams get different responses form her parents (the rudiments of communication). She also begins to learn about the interactive nature of communication – for example, her parents respond to her meaningless utterances, giving her the idea of *turntaking*.

You, then me, then you, then me... (Snow 1977)

PHONOLOGY: At (roughly) **8-20 weeks**, the child improves her voice control. She is now also beginning to use her tongue to produce softer 'comfort' sounds consisting of a consonant and a vowel ('coo', 'gaa', 'goo'): **the cooing Stage.**

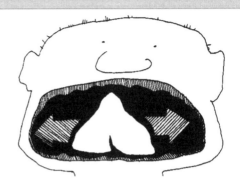

PHONOLOGY: The next stage – **age 20-50 weeks** – is spent experimenting with pitch, volume, vowel sounds,

OOOOEEEAAA

nasal sounds,

NNNNNMMMMM

and fricative sounds.

This stage is known as **VERBAL SCRIBBLING** or **'VOCAL PLAY'**. Gradually this gives way to the **Babbling Stage**, when the sounds become less varied but more frequent and stable, e.g.

AABABAADADA!

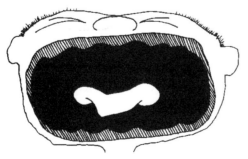

PRAGMATICS: Non-verbal language also develops a great deal in this month. At around **9 months** children use gesture and body language a great deal. This shows that the child is acquiring a good understanding of the language she cannot yet express verbally.

Finally, at **9-18 months**, comes the **Melodic Utterance Stage**, when children pick up the melody, rhythm and intonation of their mother tongue. At this point a child will sound as if she is talking despite the lack of actual words. For example, one child used the rhythm and melody of '*tum ti tum ti tumtum*' to ask for a game of 'Round and round the garden', whilst many others can be heard to copy the rise and fall intonation of *all-gone* (Crystal, 1986 p.46).

CHILD
LANGUAGE
ACQUISITION

STAGE ①NE: HOLOPHRASTIC (ONE WORD)

AGE: 12-18 months

WHAT HAPPENS: The child utters her first word. She then builds up a vocabulary of **holophrases** (single words used to convey many meanings), which can reach about 50 words. She will be able to understand about five times as many words by this time.

why are they called Holophrases, not words?

DADDY?? DADDY. DADDY!!!

Because they convey all the meaning of a phrase/sentence through body language, intonation and volume.

TYPE OF WORDS:
Short and related to the here and now – The child's everyday life:

DOGGY   POON   BALL   DINK

They are often unrecognisable as adult English words:

TOOFEEF!   BIZDA?

('One, two, three, four, five')   ('What's that?')

STAGE TWO: TWO WORD

AGE: Around 18 months

WHAT HAPPENS: This one's fairly self-explanatory: the child begins to use two words at a time. Some call this stage 'the emergence of grammar', because it is now possible for the child to choose a word order, and for us to make simple grammatical analyses of the meanings of these 'sentences' (see below).

TYPE OF UTTERANCES:

More flexible, with a range of grammatical functions e.g.

1. AN ACTION AFFECTS AN OBJECT
2. AN ACTOR PERFORMS AN ACTION
3. AN OBJECT IS GIVEN A LOCATION

> *'Make bridge'*
> *'Mommy Sleep'*
> *'Doll dere'*

However, even though it's possible to work out the grammar behind many utterances, there are still quite a few that defy definition and often understanding:

> *'Hot pretty'* *'Mummy-Daddy'* *'Teddy juice'*

As you can imagine, meaning still relies heavily on the context and a sympathetic listener.

That said, these utterances should not be seen as deficient or wanting. Even at 18 months children have grasped a great deal about English grammar: the vast majority of utterances have

the **correct syntax** (word order):   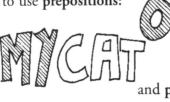   (not 'Bed my')

And children are beginning to use **prepositions**:

And **possession words:**

and **pronouns:**

AGE: 2-2 ½ years

WHAT HAPPENS: The child begins to use sentences of up to four words in length.

TYPE OF UTTERANCE: Sentences with gaps in them, where the **non-lexical** words (those without a 'dictionary meaning') like **'and'**, **'but'**, **'if'** (conjunctions), **'the'**, **'a'** (articles), **'is'**, **'has'** (auxiliary verbs), as well as endings such as **'ing'** are often omitted – hence the name 'telegraphic'.

Children combine **3-4 words** in a variety of grammatical constructions:

STATEMENTS. .

ME GOT BOAT.

ME DO DAT.

MAN KICK BALL.

IT FALL DOWN.

HIM GOT CAR

MY MOUSE EATING.

QUESTIONS. . .   **COMMANDS. . .**

WHERE DADDY GOING?

WHAT DOING IT?

PUT THAT ON THERE!

OPEN IT!

After the age of three, children's language advances in leaps and bounds.

Although massive developments happen simultaneously and are all linked together, the simplest way to examine them is by dividing them into the **four categories** of...

GRAMMAR: The structure of the language (word order, sentence types, word endings, tenses, using negatives, passives, conjunctions)

SEMANTICS: The meaning of words (the usage, growth, and comprehension of vocabulary)

PHONOLOGY: The sounds of the language (intonation, stress, pitch, tone, pronunciation)

PRAGMATICS: Everything else. Or, the ability to use language that is appropriate to the situation, the rules of conversation, (turntaking, politeness, terms of address), linguistic strategies (how to initiate a conversation, how to keep it going, how to keep someone's attention, how to get someone to do what you want and make them feel like it was their idea, and so on).

FIRST: GRAMMAR

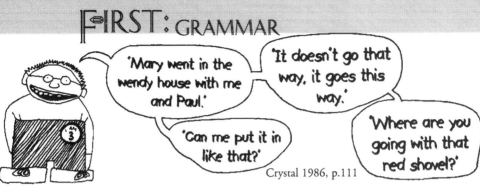

'Mary went in the wendy house with me and Paul.'

'It doesn't go that way, it goes this way.'

'Can me put it in like that?'

'Where are you going with that red shovel?'

Crystal 1986, p.111

The grammatical advance the child makes between the ages of two and three years old is astonishing. Her utterances lose their telegraphic quality, as she gradually picks up non-lexical words and word endings. Sentences also get much longer because she begins to use more than one **clause** (a separate meaningful element in a sentence). Lots of these are linked by **'and'** (**co-ordinate clauses**) and can turn into very long sentences:

Daddy have breaked the spade all up and – and – and – it broken – and he did hurt his hand on it and – and – and its gone all sore and – and... Crystal 1986, p.146

I LET GO **COS** IT HURTED ME.

I THINK **THAT** HE WILL FALL OVER.

But children also begin to experiment with other conjunctions including, 'cos', 'when', 'so', 'if' and 'after', creating subordinate clauses and expressing contrast as well as cause and effect.

However, children's errors at this stage often show that although they can readily create long complex sentences, the complicated *semantic* meanings of some conjunctions are yet to be understood properly, for example, the cause and effect implied by a 'because' clause.

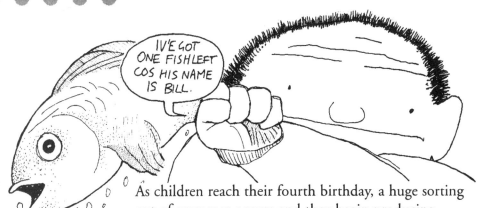

I'VE GOT ONE FISH LEFT COS HIS NAME IS BILL.

As children reach their fourth birthday, a huge sorting out of grammar occurs and they begin producing long, fluent, error-free monologues. This task is by no means easy though, and it often takes several years to overcome problems like:

'It just got <u>bro<u>ken</u></u>'	*(irregular past tenses)*
'That's <u>more</u> better'	*(comparatives v superlatives)*
'A girl fell over in play group and hurt herself on a chair and <u>it</u> was bleeding'	*(pronouns)*
'I'm bored <u>at</u> shopping'	*(prepositions)*
'The lake is freezing <u>if</u> I want to go skating'	*(conditional meaning)*

This sorting out of grammar continues well into the early school years. At around the ages of **7-8 years**, for example, children begin to use more complicated, subtle sentence connectors:

FOR INSTANCE
WHETHER
OF COURSE
THOUGH
ACTUALLY
WAY
REALLY ANYWAY
FORTUNATELY
OTHERWISE
OBVIOUSLY
ALTHOUGH
HOWEVER

It also takes until the age of eight or nine for children to learn that many sentences that look or sound similar have different meanings. The most obvious example of this is **passives**. Before a certain stage in their development, children seem to interpret all passive sentences as active ones. We can tell this from experiments that linguists call **elicited imitation**, in which the researcher asks a child to try to repeat exactly what she says. Here are some examples of what happens:

NOW REPEAT AFTER ME: 'THE OWL WHO EATS CANDY RUNS FAST'.

OWL EAT CANDY AND HE RUN FAST.

OK, NOW SAY 'I CAN SEE THREE MICE'.

I SEE THREE MOUSES.

I ♥ PSYCHO-LINGUIS-TICS.

These examples all show children understanding the meaning, but being unable to use the relevant construction. However, when a 2½-year-old child is asked to repeat a passive sentence, we can clearly see that he does not understand the meaning:

OK, GOOD. NOW SAY 'THE CAT WAS CHASED BY THE DOG'.

THE CAT IS CHASING THE DOG.

SIGH... THIS KID IS A GENIUS.

(Slobin and Welsh, 1967)

CHILD LANGUAGE ACQUISITION

Two interesting features to study are QUESTIONS and NEGATIVES. Children use simple versions of both in their first year, but their usage gradually becomes more and more refined:

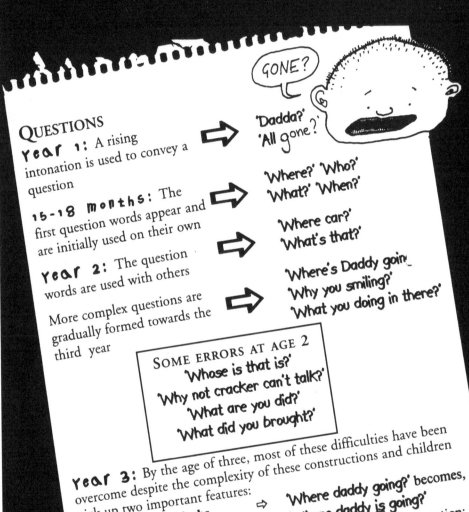

QUESTIONS

Year 1: A rising intonation is used to convey a question

➡ 'Dadda?'
'All gone?'

'GONE?'

15-18 months: The first question words appear and are initially used on their own

➡ 'Where?' 'Who?'
'What?' 'When?'

Year 2: The question words are used with others

➡ 'Where car?'
'What's that?'

More complex questions are gradually formed towards the third year

➡ 'Where's Daddy goin'_
'Why you smiling?'
'What you doing in there?'

SOME ERRORS AT AGE 2
'Whose is that is?'
'Why not cracker can't talk?'
'What are you did?'
'What did you brought?'

Year 3: By the age of three, most of these difficulties have been overcome despite the complexity of these constructions and children pick up two important features:

1. **Auxiliary Verbs** ⇨ 'Where daddy going?' becomes, 'Where daddy is going?'

2. **The Inversion Rule** ⇨ 'He is sad' becomes a question: 'Is he sad?'

Unfortunately, they now have to learn that this rule doesn't always apply - e.g. you don't say 'Went he to town?'

NEGATIVES

Year 1: Gesture is used i.e. child shakes his head, frowns, turns his back.

18 months: Negative Holophrases used.

'No,' 'Not,' 'Bye,' 'Gone,' or even 'N-N-N.'

Year 2 -2½: Negatives used at the beginning and end of two word sentences.

'Not there,' 'Not mine,' 'No sat,' 'Running no.'

Year 3: Negatives are now used in the middle of sentences.

'You no do that,' 'I no want to go to bed,' 'Mummy no got it,'

The verbs **can't, won't** and **don't** appear (used only in the negative for a while) 'Me can't do that,' 'I don't know,' 'Her won't sit down properly,'

Around year 4: Negative words and endings are used much more accurately: 'n't' is used with more verbs **'She isn't going,'** and **'not'** replaces **no** more often: **'You've not got one,'** instead of ' **You've no got one'**

Years 5/6/7: Subtle negatives like 'hardly' and 'scarcely' are picked up and greater understanding of indirect refusal/denial develops e.g, 'It'll be tea time shortly,' and 'You've just had one,' actually mean:

'No, you can't have a biscuit.'

NEXT: SEMANTICS

Semantics seems at first like the easiest area of child language acquisition to study and quantify: studies of vocabulary growth are one of the oldest lines of research, and you'd think that it would be easy to check what children understand by examining what they say and respond to.

● ● ● ● ● ● ●

However, a conversation with a young child soon shows that quite a few words just don't mean the same to her. If a child uses a word, it does not necessarily follow that she understands its adult meaning.

Children's errors are very important to linguists since they give an indication of their thought processes and developmental progress.

1. OVEREXTENSION
(EXTENDING THE MEANING)

MOO COWS

2. UNDEREXTENSION
(CONTRACTING THE MEANING)

NOT SHOES.   SHOES.

3. MISMATCH
(CHOOSING A SEEMINGLY UNRELATED MEANING)

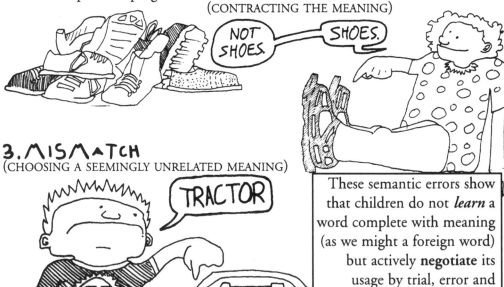

TRACTOR

These semantic errors show that children do not *learn* a word complete with meaning (as we might a foreign word) but actively **negotiate** its usage by trial, error and observation.

Studying comprehension of vocabulary is made more difficult because children, like adults, often act upon non-linguistic messages (gesture/ body language, context, past experience) even if they don't understand the words.

FOR EXAMPLE, Clark, Hutcheson and Van Buren (1974) observed a boy named Adam carrying strawberries to his father. After a while his mother asked,

"Don't you think that's enough?"

And he promptly offered her a strawberry.

- (He based his response on the non-linguistic context, in which a
- request for a strawberry is likely.) The point is that if she had
- asked, '**May I have one?**' everyone would have assumed that he
- had understood perfectly.

- So, after the two-word stage, estimates of vocabulary growth and
- comprehension become very vague. The only thing that is certain is
- that children learn amazingly fast. It is not really surprising that it
- takes time to work out exactly what adults' words mean, if you
- consider the complexities of meaning in English.

TO BEGIN WITH

there are words that mean more than one thing. Take *fare/fair/fayre*: this one word (soundwise) means <u>the cost</u> when you are travelling on a bus, <u>light coloured</u> when you are talking about hair, <u>just and equal</u> when you are sharing out sweets, <u>beautiful</u> when storybooks describe princesses and <u>a circus with candy floss</u>. To add to this, it crops up as part of phrases like *'fair and square'*, *'fair enough'* and *'fair play'*.

And to make matters worse, lots of things have more than one name:

And you can't sit down with a textbook and learn one word at a time; it all happens at once. For this reason, things with obvious differences between them (like 'shoe' and 'sock') present little problem, but words with more subtle distinguishing characteristics can be very confusing.

Surprisingly, 'opposites' often cause trouble – *'hot'* and *'cold'*, *'tall'* and *'short'*, *'big'* and *'small'*, *'before'* and *'after'* – because they are about the same thing: *'hot'* and *'cold'*, for example, are both *about* temperature, and they both go in exactly the same place in a sentence:

MONDAY **TUESDAY**

AND NOW: PHONOLOGY

Children's ability to pronounce words and to use the English sound system develops much slower than comprehension: a one-year-old child, for example, can recognise perhaps 50 words but pronounce only about 3 consonants and a vowel.

There's lots of research which shows that a child's own pronunciation does not reflect what she knows about the adult sound system, and that it is perhaps quite different from what she thinks she's saying:

(Berko & Brown 1960)

Children's acquisition of phonology is gradual and occurs step by step: they start with a restricted set of words and gradually increase their repertoire, just as they start with one-word utterances and slowly build up longer and longer sentences.

In the first couple of years, there are obvious patterns to the way children alter certain sounds:

1. GROUPS OF CONSONANTS ARE AVOIDED

E.G.	'SKY'	'GY'
	'PLAY'	'PEY

2. UNSTRESSED SOUNDS OR SYLLABLES ARE DROPPED (OFTEN AT THE ENDS OF WORDS)

E.G.	'BANANA'	'NANA'
	'CAT'	'CA'

3. SOUNDS ARE MADE MORE LIKE NEIGHBOURING ONES

E.G.	'YELLOW'	'LELLOW'
	'BOTTLE'	'BO BO'
	'DOG'	'GOG'

4. CERTAIN SOUNDS ARE SUBSTITUTED FOR OTHERS

E.G.	'RED'	'WED'
	'SEE'	'TEE'
	'GONE'	'DON'

fricatives (sounds produced by friction between vocal organs)

velar sounds (made by the tongue and the back of the mouth) are replaced by alveolar sounds (made by the tongue and the front of the mouth)

Something often heard around the second year is **reduplication**. This means turning words like bottle, water and window into...

BU-BU, WO-WO and NU-NU

No one is certain why children do this, but David Crystal has suggested that the repetition and simplified pronunciation in these words helps children to recognise and learn them bit by bit (Crystal 1986 p.86). Children also replace new, difficult words with phonologically similar ones as a kind of stand-in whilst they're learning the correct one.

KITCHENS!

And a child's pronunciation of the same word can often vary a great deal from day-to-day or even hour-to-hour. For example one child produced over ten different forms of the word '**pen**' in just half an hour.

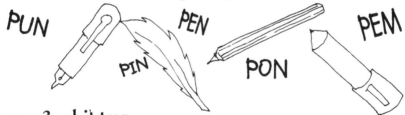

PUN   PEN   PEM   PIN   PON

By age 3, children

✍ Have usually grasped twice as many consonants and nearly all the vowels
✍ Are using words of three syllables
✍ Are using emphasis of key words

YOU GOT A **LITTLE** CROCODILE, I GOT A **BIG** ONE.

(Crystal 1986)

However, there are still some problem areas by **age 4**. The main one is consonant clusters (several consonants next to each other, as in *'spin'* and *'judge'*).

They will have begun to use them in some words, e.g. **break'**, and **'box'** (bocks) but consonants can be joined in over 300 different ways in English and it takes another couple of years to fully master them all.

Some other difficult sounds are:

Later development: By **age 5**, most of these things are no longer a problem and single consonants only cause children trouble in long or unfamiliar words. **INTONATION** is one of the earliest and also one of the latest phonological features to be tackled. It is the first sign of the mother tongue coming out of babble and one of the first strategies to be used to make up for a lack of grammar.

So children of **about 12 months** quickly pick up the formal patterns of intonation, e.g., use a rising intonation to form a question.

But, it still takes until the early teens to grasp all the meanings behind these patterns. The first researcher to show this was Allan Cruttenden (1974) who looked at the way British Radio/TV announcers read out the football results. . .

LIVERPOOL 3 EVERTON 2

(As soon as they say the second team's name you can tell whether it's a draw, a home win or an away win).

He recorded sets of results just missing off the final score, e.g.

FORFAR 3... STRANRAER ...

(He used Scottish teams in his research in Manchester to avoid team loyalties impairing judgement).

He then played the tape to both adults and children asking them to predict the result (draw/home/away). **Every adult he asked got them right**, whereas seven-year-olds were hardly able to do it at all. Even the oldest children (11-year-olds) still hadn't reached adult competence. **Only 1 child out of 28 got them all right**. The interesting thing about this research is that it applies to everyday English, for example, the difference between

'She dressed, and fed the baby'   'She dressed and fed the baby'

is shown by punctuation on paper but is signalled in spoken language solely by intonation and pauses. The *italics* used in written language also stand in for spoken intonation. Compare these two sentences:

Cruttenden showed that even children approaching secondary school are still learning about how adult tone of voice affects meaning.

'John gave a book to *Jim*, and he gave one to *Mary*'   'John gave a book to Jim, and he gave one to *Mary*'

FINALLY: PRAGMATICS

An understanding of how and when to use words is, of course, just as important as the understanding of the words themselves. Linguists have not yet gone as far as to lay down distinct stages in pragmatic development, but it is plain to see that such an understanding develops surprisingly early. The two following conversations taken from the research of P. Fletcher (1985) show the massive development between the ages of two and four:

2-YEAR-OLD CHILD: Ball. Kick. Kick. Daddy kick.

MOTHER: That's right, you have to kick it, don't you?

CHILD: **Mmm. Um. Um. Kick hard. Only kick hard. Our play that. On floor. Our play that on floor. Now. Our play that on floor. No that. Now.**

MOTHER: All right.

4-YEAR-OLD CHILD:
Hester be fast asleep, Mummy.

MOTHER: She was tired.

CHILD: **And why did her have two sweets, Mummy?**

MOTHER: Because you each had two, that's why. She had the same as you. Ooh dear, now what?

CHILD: **Daddy didn't give me two in the end.**

MOTHER: Yes, he did.

CHILD: **He didn't.**

P. Fletcher 1985 pg. 64

As you can see, the conversation of the two-year-old is repetitive, erratic, disjointed and she is at times unaware of her audience – she talks to herself. The older child is quite fluent, she can initiate a conversation, obtain and hold the attention of the listener, handle turntaking conventions and elaborate when asked to.

Between 3 and 5 the child develops further pragmatic skills such as:
● The use of forms of address, '**Excuse me, Mrs...**'
● Politeness markers, '**please**', '**sorry**', etc.
● How to make indirect requests. **'Do you want that piece of cake, Daddy?'**
● And, how to deal with difficult negotiations. M. McTear (1985) reported a conversation between two kids that took 60 turns just for one to convince the other that he should pass him some scissors.

OK. That's the simple bit over with. (It's a lot easier to describe what kids say than it is to work out how on earth they do it...) So here comes the tough bit.

PART TWO:

THE⊕RIES ⊕ LANGUAGE ACQUISITION

The question of how children learn language has occupied the minds of scholars and clever people since time immemorial, especially because many have believed that the study of child language acquisition would reveal clues about the origins of human language as a whole. Early experiments were conducted by the ancient Egyptians, the Roman emperors and even Plato dedicated one of his dialogues to the subject.

More recently, the behaviourist **B.F. Skinner** wrote a book called **Verbal behaviour** (1957), in which he described his theory of language acquisition.

Basically, Skinner had been performing experiments on rats and pigeons and had discovered that they could be taught to perform all sorts of tasks so long as these tasks were broken down into stages, and the rats/pigeons were repeatedly rewarded for 'correct' actions.

E.g., a rat in a box gradually learned to press a lever because it received a food pellet every time it did, and then gradually to press it only when a light was showing, because it only got the reward when the light was on. Skinner took this research and around it formed his **OPERANT CONDITIONING THEORY**.

Skinner then applied this theory directly to human learning, claiming that children learn language through a simple process of

IMITAION and REINFORCEMENT

In other words, a child who needs food might say

to his parents, because he has heard such a phrase used in this context before (**imitation**) and would then be rewarded (**reinforcement**) by being passed the food. Or, a child on seeing an iceberg might say

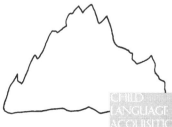

having heard such a word in that context before (**imitation**) and be rewarded (**reinforcement**) by a parent saying:

'Yes that's right, good girl.'

Skinner claimed that no complicated internal mechanisms were needed for language and that a child learning language was virtually no different from a rat learning to press levers.

'The basic processes and relations which give verbal behaviour its special characteristics are now fairly well understood. Much of the experimental work responsible for this advance has been carried out on other species, but the results have proved to be surprisingly free of species restrictions. Recent work has shown that the methods can be extended to human behaviour without serious modifications.'
(Skinner 1957 p.3)

1. DEVELOPMENTAL MILESTONES:

First of all, kids all over the world learn language at roughly the same speed regardless of sex, race, culture or mother tongue (and there are some pretty major differences in attitudes towards teaching children across the globe. For instance in some parts of the world, children aren't really spoken to directly until they are able to reply coherently). **If Skinner's hypothesis were correct, children ought to learn language at different rates according to these factors.**

2. LOGICAL MISTAKES:
If children learn language by imitating their parents, why do they create words that no adults would ever have said to them?

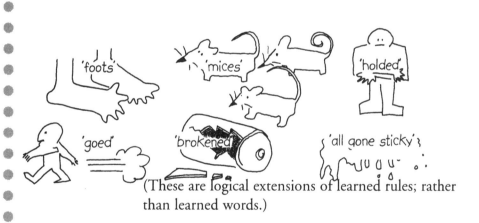

(These are logical extensions of learned rules; rather than learned words.)

3. EXCEPTIONS:
One of the most convincing arguments against the imitation theory is that children who can't speak, but can hear, acquire normal understanding of speech. Eric Lenneburg (1962) researched the case of a boy like this who, for neuromuscular reasons, was unable to speak and so could not imitate adults or have his utterances reinforced, yet he had normal comprehension of language.

4. CRITICAL PERIOD: There have been occasional cases of '**Wild Children**' who have been deprived of normal contact with humans and have therefore never acquired language. Some have been discovered at a young age and have rapidly caught up on language development. Those cases discovered as teenagers, however, rarely manage much more than a few odd words, even in the face of intensive training. This suggests that there is a limited time (critical period) in which children can acquire language.

Genie, discovered at age 13 in the 1970s, had no language because her parents hadn't spoken to her and had punished her if she made a sound. She had been confined in a chicken house and denied social contact. Despite years of teaching from psycholinguists, she never grasped the grammar that all normal five-year-olds use as the following utterances show: *'No more take wax'* and *'Another house have dog'*

This implies that there is more to language acquisition than imitation and reinforcement (processes with no time restriction).

5. CARETAKER REINFORCEMENT: If children learn correct vocabulary usage, pronunciation and grammar from their parents, then their parents ought to be correcting them on these things all the time.

In fact, research shows that parents reinforce not linguistically correct, but truthful utterances, even if they are grammatically incorrect or badly pronounced.

CHILD
LANGUAGE
ACQUISITION

It seems to be *truth value* rather than well-formed syntax that chiefly governs explicit verbal reinforcement by parents – which renders mildly paradoxical the fact that the usual product of such a training schedule is an adult whose speech is highly grammatical but not notably truthful

(R. Brown, C. Cazden and U. Bellugi 1969)

In 1973, another researcher, Katherine Nelson, found that children at the one-word stage whose mothers did correct them based on word choice and pronunciation actually advanced more slowly than those with mothers who were 'generally accepting'.

6. RESISTANCE TO CORRECTION: If kids revise their language use based on reinforcement and correction from their parents, why are they utterly impervious to correction?

(McNeill 1963)

7. FUNCTIONS OF LANGUAGE: Skinner's theory assumes that the child has two purposes for learning language:

1. Getting what she wants.

2. Getting attention or a 'pat on the back'.

Unfortunately, Skinner did not account for the truckload of other functions that have since been pointed out. For example, he didn't think about what David Crystal calls the **PHONOLOGICAL** function of language: using language purely for the love of the sound of it, as in many religious chants, pop songs and much poetry. Children invent rhymes and sayings simply because they enjoy the sound of the words.

On top of which there are the following:

1. INSTRUMENTAL: Language used to satisfy material needs

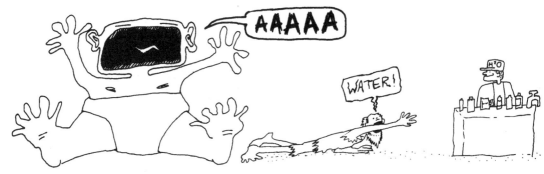

2. REGULATORY: Language used to control others
(order them around)

(As it happens, these two functions account for both the purposes assumed by Skinner.)

3. INTERACTIONAL: Language with no actual meaning as such, whose purpose is to maintain friendly relationships – filling an awkward silence or starting off a conversation.

4. PERSONAL: Emotional language which releases stress, involuntary responses to pain, fear, beauty etc., as well as expressing 'the self' – identity and social grouping

5. HEURISTIC: Language seeking information

6. IMAGINATIVE: The language of creative writing, poetry and many children's games, which involve the creation of another world

7. REPRESENTATIONAL: Language that communicates information or ideas (the majority of the language used in this book for example)

8. PERFORMATIVE: Language that attempts to control reality (curses, charms, magic, prayers, etc.)

M.A.K Halliday

N.B. Lots of language fulfils more than one of these functions.

Well, we've been pretty damning about this theory, but we now want to make it clear that most of these objections relate to the acquisition of grammatical structures. It is likely that imitation plays an important part in semantic development when children are amassing vocabulary and also in the acquisition of sounds. Reinforcement, too, is important, but as general positive encouragement for the child, not a rigorous teaching mechanism.

Recently more and more researchers have been taking an interest in what is known as:

CARETAKER LANGUAGE

(How we talk to kids)

Everybody adapts their language while talking to children and babies. Even four-year-olds do it when addressing their little brothers/sisters.

Here's what we do:

1. PHONOLOGY

✐ We separate phrases more distinctly, leaving longer pauses between them

✐ We speak more s-l-o-w-l-y

✐ We use exaggerated 'singsong' intonation, which helps to <u>emphasise</u> key words, e.g.

And <u>to exaggerate the difference between questions, statements and commands</u>

✐ We generally use a <u>higher and wider pitch range</u>.

2. SEMANTICS

✏️ We use far more <u>restricted</u> <u>vocabulary</u> (generally avoiding astro-physics, quantum mechanics, and the meaning of life and plumping for concrete things related to the here and now).

✏️ Also, the most noticeable feature of baby talk, we use a more <u>simplified</u> <u>vocabulary</u> such as

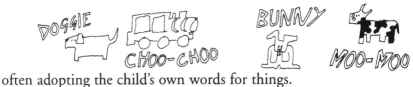

often adopting the child's own words for things.

3. GRAMMAR

✎ We use fewer verbs and fewer tenses of those verbs.

✎ We tend to use much shorter sentences (3.7 seconds on average compared to 8.4 seconds with an adult, according to the research of Philips, 1973)

✎ We use fewer incomplete sentences and a more restricted range of sentence patterns, such as *'where's. . .'* and *'there's a. . .'*

Adult:	Where's Ben's jumper?
Child:	*Here!*
Adult:	Where's Ben's nose?
Child:	*Here!*
Adult:	Where's Ben's stomach?
Child:	*Here!*
Adult:	Umm. . .
Child:	*Where's Ben's knees?*

✎We use more simple sentences and fewer complex sentences and passives.

✎We also use more questions and tag questions that draw responses from the child, e.g.

'That's a nice colour, isn't it?'

'Daddy's gone out, hasn't he?'

Anyone who has tried to learn a foreign language will instantly recognise the benefits of being presented with this slower, clearer, simpler version to start with. Compare school French tapes:

'My name is Jean. What is your name?'

'My name is Chantal. I am 12 years old. How old are you?'

AND NOW A SONG FROM MY PERSONAL FAVOURITES YES THAT'S RIGHT IF YOU GUESSED IT IT'S JOHNNY BAGUETTE AND THE PURPLE BRICKLAYERS WITH THEIR LATEST TOP SMASH HIT "MY BABY" DON'T TOUCH THAT DIAL!!!

To the high-speed gabble of a French radio station.

However, it is important not to overestimate how much we simplify our language: not all caretaker speech is simple, short, slow and repetitious, there is still lots of variety in caretakerese and the parents' language always remains at a higher level than that of the child, thus continually stretching him.

4. PRAGMATICS

And, recent research seems to suggest that it isn't what parents actually say (whether specific words or structures), but the interchange between the adult and the child (the pragmatics) that is most important. Again, this ties in with foreign language learning: it is so much easier to learn French by talking to a 'real' French person than by repeating simple sentences from a tape.

Here are some of the Pragmatic features of Caretaker language:

✎ A great deal of <u>gesture</u> and <u>warm</u> <u>body</u> <u>language</u>

✎ <u>Fewer</u> <u>utterances</u> <u>per</u> <u>turn</u>, i.e., we may say the same thing to a child as to an adult, but we break it down into smaller bits, stopping frequently for the child to have her say

✎ <u>Supportive</u> <u>language</u> – when a child says something partly unintelligible, adults often **echo** the utterance replacing the unclear bit with a question to encourage them to repeat it.

I going owa nah

You're going where?

Baby highchair

Adults also copy and **expand upon** children's utterances – usually to clarify the utterance based upon the context.

It is as yet uncertain exactly how important specific features like these are, however the sum of all these factors does seem to aid development and create a warm supportive environment for the child to learn in. ● ● ● ● ● ●

Baby is in the highchair

(Brown & Bellugi 1964

We are also certain that language acquisition is not as simple as parents just 'teaching' children language through imitation and reinforcement. It is the children who are the active ones.

So, to get back to the point, the problem with Skinner's theory is that it just doesn't take into account all the functions of language or children's massive creativity with language.

Also, it's about rats and pigeons, not children.

LANGUAGE ACQUISITION DEVICE

In 1957 Noam Chomsky (arguably the most influential linguist of this century, mentioned in the History chapter) pointed this out in his review of Skinner's theory:

He also set out his own ideas on the subject.
He began with the idea that

> *'The person who has acquired knowledge of a language has internalised a system of rules that relate sound and meaning in a particular way.'*

Thus he wasn't looking at why a child says 'More juice' (which could conceivably relate to Skinner's Operant Conditioning Theory) but at why a child can eventually understand a sentence that he has never heard before such as

'I was eaten alive by my giant ant.'

He also stated that it would be impossible to learn an entire grammar based on the limited experience of a small child. So he hypothesised that children must have some kind of headstart or *rich internal structure* to help them, i.e., **children have an innate capacity for language learning**:

an L.A.D. (Language Acquisition Device) inside their heads.

 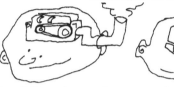 

Nearly all linguists today agree that there must be 'something innate' inside a child. The argument now concerns exactly what is innate. There are two main sides:

CONTENT   PRIMARY LINGUISTIC DATA (SPEECH AROUND CHILD)   PROCESS

INNATE, SPECIFIC KNOWLEDGE ABOUT LANGUAGE → INTERNAL GRAMMAR → SPEECH

«L·A·D»

INNATE PUZZLE SOLVING EQUIPMENT → INTERNAL GRAMMAR → SPEECH

Chomsky's theory

attributes tacit knowledge of linguistic universals to the child. It proposes that the child approaches the data (LANGUAGE AROUND HIM) with the presumption that they are drawn from a language of a certain antedecedently well-defined type, his problem being to determine which of the (humanly) possible languages is that of the community in which he is placed. (Chomsky 1965, p.27)

Whereas the process approach endows the child with an innate *hypothesis making device* with which to process language.
The main alternative theory is,

LITTLE NOAM

A PSYCHOLINGUISTIC MODEL

Jean Piaget's (1896-1980) theory was that cognitive maturation (intellectual development) and language development go hand in hand.

He argued that a child's acquisition of a linguistic structure depends upon his understanding of the concepts behind it. One of the key elements he discussed was **egocentrism.**

That is to say, to begin with children view themselves as the centre of the universe and other objects only in relation to themselves. This is why the peek-a-boo game works. (From the baby's point of view if she can't see you, you're not there and so when you reappear it comes as a pleasant surprise).

It is around the age of **18 months** that children begin to realise that things have an existence that has nothing to do with their interaction with them.

Linguists have argued that the massive growth in vocabulary that occurs around this time, may be a result of children finding names for things they now realise exist.

Another interesting example of the link between intelligence and language is **seriation**:

Before children have developed the cognitive ability to contrast sizes they cannot use comparative structures. In practice, this means that children who can't line up a bunch of sticks in order from long to short also can't use terms like 'longer' and 'shorter'; they are restricted to only 'long' and 'short'.

Piaget also emphasised the activity on the part of the child, which is something most linguists now see as an essential part of language learning.

Several researchers have found that children actually go through linguistic drills alone before going to sleep.

Ruth Weir (1972) recorded her son's pre-sleep dialogues in her book *Language in the Crib*. For example:

'Block; yellow block; Look at the yellow block. What colour? What colour blanket? What colour Mop? What colour glass?'

This transcript shows Anthony actively practising and correcting himself on his grammar and vocabulary.

So, as you can see, Piaget's theory does hold true for some examples; however, these are largely in the first 18 months. As the child grows up and both language and thought become more complicated, it becomes very hard to work out the exact links between the two, so we still don't know to what extent they are related. The relationship between language and thought will be discussed further in the next chapter, but as far as this chapter's concerned, its...

chapter three:

SEX AND POWER

Part 1
SEX AND SPEECH pg. 86

- ❤ Do men and women talk differently?
- ❤ Is one gender's language 'better' than the other?

Part 2
BIAS AND LANGUAGE pg. 106

- ❤ Is the English language inherently prejudiced against women?
- ❤ Is it biased against anybody else?
  Black people? Disabled people?
- ❤ Why is it? And what can we do about it?

Part 3
POWER AND LANGUAGE pg. 130

- ❤ What is the relationship between language and thought?
- ❤ How can language be used to persuade/manipulate people?

IS THERE SUCH A THING AS

'WOMEN'S LANGUAGE'?

Well...

Have you noticed that people always investigate whether there's a 'Women's language' or whether **women** speak differently? Don't you think it's a bit sexist to always treat us like the oddballs?

Well...

The question itself is biased. Women are half of the population, so why pick **men's** speech as the standard to judge by?

Well, the thing is, we live in a patriarchy, and throughout history men have had the power.

The linguists and dictionary writers were men. **So, they took the way they spoke to be the norm.** Any differences between how they spoke and how women did showed a deviance from the norm by the women.

MALE AS NORMAL, FEMALE AS ABNORMAL

Until recently, very little solid research was actually done into the differences between women's and men's speech. But that didn't mean linguists had nothing to say on the matter. Since at least the 17th century, women have been blamed for unwelcome changes to the language, or expressions linguists disliked.

The first 'dictionary of hard words' was in fact aimed at *'Ladies, Gentlewomen, or any other unskilful persons'*. In this century, Otto Jesperson (1922 p.246) declared that *'There is a danger of the language becoming vague and insipid if we are to content ourselves with women's expressions'*. And, that women were not as effective in their speech as men due to *'their preference for...veiled and indirect expressions'*.

Later in this century when research began in earnest, the questions asked were often biased.

SOCIETY'S BELIEFS ABOUT WOMEN HAVE OFTEN AFFECTED THE RESEARCH, SO THAT IT IS NOT THE SPEAKER'S LANGUAGE, BUT THEIR SEX THAT IS JUDGED.

THERE IS A KIND OF CIRCULAR LOGIC HERE THAT SAYS:

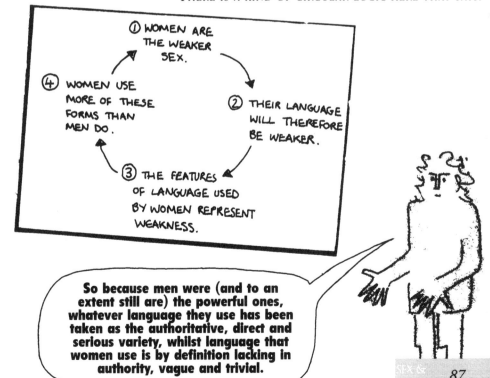

① WOMEN ARE THE WEAKER SEX.

② THEIR LANGUAGE WILL THEREFORE BE WEAKER.

③ THE FEATURES OF LANGUAGE USED BY WOMEN REPRESENT WEAKNESS.

④ WOMEN USE MORE OF THESE FORMS THAN MEN DO.

So because men were (and to an extent still are) the powerful ones, whatever language they use has been taken as the authoritative, direct and serious variety, whilst language that women use is by definition lacking in authority, vague and trivial.

So what are these differences between men's and women's speech?

Well, the first study people always refer to is *Language and Woman's Place* (1975) by ROBIN LAKOFF. Although aspects of her study have been criticised since, it was ground- breaking in its time.

Her theory was that all children's first language is 'Women's Language', learnt from their mums before they go to school. Once there, boys learn 'rough talk' and by the time children are about 10, there are two languages. Boys have 'unlearned' women's language and begun speaking the language of power, whereas girls continue to use the weaker women's language.

How is women's language 'weaker'?

According to Lakoff, having to use women's language *'Submerges a woman's personal identity, by denying her the means of expressing herself strongly...and encouraging expressions that suggest triviality in subject matter and uncertainty about it...The ultimate effect of these discrepancies is that women are systematically denied access to power, on the grounds that they are not capable of holding it as demonstrated by their linguistic behaviour along with other aspects of their behaviour.'*

(Lakoff 1975 p.7)

1. WOMEN'S WORDS

❤ 'Women's work words': words related to women's specific interests, e.g., sewing terms and fine colour definition words like *mauve, lavender, ecru,* and *aquamarine.* Supposedly, women's vocabulary includes 'trivial' words like these because they are relegated to decisions about such unimportant subjects, whilst men have more need of vocabulary to do with work and the 'real world'

❤ Adjectives of approval: according to Lakoff, there are two groups of these, neutral and women-only: neutral ones (like *great, terrific, cool, neat*) may be used by men or women. The women-only adjectives include *'adorable', 'charming', 'sweet', 'lovely',* and *'divine'.* For a man to use these could be *damaging to his reputation.*

❤ Weak expletives *instead of swear words:* (e.g. *'oh dear'* instead of *'shit'*) According to Lakoff, women are forbidden to display anger and to express opinions forcefully, reinforcing men's position of power.

❤ Using the intensifier 'so' inconclusively: e.g. 'I like him *so* much.' (So much *that what?*) This is again supposed to be a way of avoiding strong statements or committing yourself to an opinion.

2. WOMEN'S GRAMMAR

❤ Extensive use of tag questions: (e.g. *It's hot in here, isn't it?*) to add uncertainty to a statement, so that the speaker doesn't impose her point of view on anyone.

❤ Use of 'hedges': (i.e. 'kind of', 'sort of', 'you know') which she claimed punctuate speech with uncertainty.

❤ Use of 'hypercorrect' grammar: Women are more likely to comply with grammatical rules, e.g., by avoiding using *'ain't'* and double negatives: *'I didn't have none'.*

3. WOMEN'S INTONATION (PHONOLOGY)

❤ **Use of a rising intonation (usually associated with questions) in the context of a statement:**
Q: *'When shall we eat?"*
A: *'Oh, in about half an hour?'* (As if to say *'In about half an hour if that's okay with you, I can always change it if you disagree'.*)
Again, Lakoff says, this implies weakness and uncertainty.

❤ **Speaking in Italics:** women use exaggerated intonation and stress (rather than volume, expletives, etc.) for emphasis ('I *really wish* you wouldn't *do* that'), which is apparently another way of expressing uncertainty.

4. HIGH LEVELS OF POLITENESS

❤ **Women are careful to use polite forms :** (i.e., 'please', 'thank you') and to uphold other social conventions.

❤ **They are more likely to use implication rather than directness:** *'It's cold in here'* meaning *'Why don't you close the window?'* or *'You borrowed my coat'* or *'Let's go to another room'* or *'You're going to make me catch cold'.*

❤**More frequent use of euphemism:** to avoid indelicate subjects

❤ AND FINALLY,
women don't tell jokes.

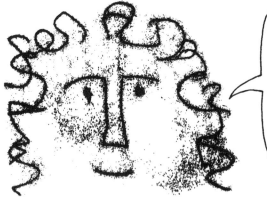

Lakoff goes on to explain that to succeed in the male-dominated real world, a woman must become bilingual and face the difficulty of shifting between women's language (for situations when she needs to be taken seriously as a woman) and men's (for being taken seriously as a person — college, job interviews, etc.)

But was she right? Does 'Women's Language' exist?

Well, as Lakoff's theories were not based on controlled experiments or hard evidence but on her personal observations, maybe we should look at some more research on the subject:

First, 'Women's Words

WOMEN'S WORK WORDS: Her claim that women have more vocabulary relating to their interests seems indisputable. It's inevitable that a person's interests and occupation will affect their vocabulary: Doctors use more medical terms than fishermen who use more angling terms than most other people...

Mira Komarovsky (1962) examined the activities and related language of 58 working-class American couples. She found that the two sexes did have different interests and topics of conversation: The women spoke to other women about **family** and **personal matters** whilst men spoke to other men about **money, business, sport, work** and **local politics.**

What does of course vary is each individual woman or man's area of interest. A male textile designer would obviously have more vocabulary to do with colour and sewing than most women.

There isn't much research on whether Lakoff was right about those specific words, but...

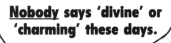

Nobody says 'divine' or 'charming' these days.

Exactly, they're quite dated now, as they're the kind of words that go in and out of fashion quickly.

However numerous linguists have recorded the different vocabulary used by different social groups. Just as young people use different approval adjectives to old people, it is likely that women and men use different terms because they are fitting in with their sex group.

What is interesting is her saying that *'a man's reputation may be damaged'* if he uses the 'women only' adjectives. It shows society's regard for women: it doesn't actually matter what the specific adjectives are, if they tend to be used by women, they will be perceived as weak, and inappropriate for men to use.

> Yeah, there's nothing that makes 'charming' or 'divine' inherently weaker or emptier than 'cool' or 'neat'. They are seen that way because women use them.

SWEARING There is little empirical evidence on female/male use of swear words. What there is, is research to show the strong stereotype we have of men swearing more:

Cheris Kramer (1974) looked at cartoons in *The New Yorker* and found that the male characters swore far more than the females. She then asked students to guess the sex of the character by looking at isolated speech bubbles. She found that students commented that swearing distinguished the male from the female speech and that at least 66% got the character's sex right.

> So that's it for 'Women's Words'. Next, **here's 'Women's Phonology'**

Research shows that there are some phonological differences between women's and men's speech. Here's what we know:

1. There is a biological basis for women's voices being high pitched and men's being lower. But research (e.g., Mattingly 1969) shows that this difference is too great to be explained only by physical differences. **This suggests that we modify the pitch of our voices to fit in with what is considered normal for our sex.** In fact Luchsinger and Arnold (1965) claim that the voices of some men who are born deaf don't break because they have never heard the sex differences in pitch.

2. **Women and men use intonation in different ways.** Men seem to use a smaller pitch range: Ruth Brend's (1975) study shows that men use three levels of intonation, whilst women use four (the fourth being a higher level).

3. **Women are more likely to use correct (standard) pronunciation** than men of the same class. (See p. 163-165)

TAG QUESTIONS

This is an extremely controversial one. Researchers disagree both about, whether women or men use more tags and what using those tags shows.

♥ *Dubois and Crouch (1975)* recorded speech at an academic conference and found that **the men used tags far more than the women.**

♥ *Pamela Fishman (1980)* recorded 52 hours of conversation between young American couples. She found that **the women in her study used three times as many yes/no and 'tag' questions as the men.** But, she proposed that this was not because they were uncertain and tentative as Lakoff suggested, but because the women were generally the ones trying to keep the conversation going and they used questions to get a response from the men.

♥ In her study, *Janet Holmes (1984)* found that women used slightly more tag questions than men, but she distinguished between two varieties of tag:

'**Modal Tags**' which are 'speaker orientated' because they seek information the speaker wants, e.g. *'The programmes on at 8 p.m., isn't it?'* and '**Affective Tags**' which are 'addressee orientated' because they show the speaker's concern for the addressee, either by softening a negative comment *('softeners'):* *'That was pretty silly, wasn't it?'* Or by showing solidarity with the addressee and drawing him into the conversation ('**Facilitative tags**'): *'I much prefer that colour, don't you?'* Holmes found that

61% of Modal tags were used by men, whilst
75% of Facilitative tags were used by women.

Suggesting the same as Fishman: **women tend to use tags to keep a conversation running smoothly, not to show uncertainty.**

Several researchers have commented on how complex this relationship is between a feature of language and 'what it shows'. Most now reject the idea that there can be a direct one-to-one relationship between a feature of language and its purpose (e.g. tag questions show uncertainty). **The same feature serves different functions depending on the context in which it's used.**

<u>Dale Spender</u> suggests that features like **intensifiers** *('so', 'such')* and **qualifiers** *('perhaps', 'maybe')* are taken as evidence of uncertainty when used by women and of certainty and authority when men use them: *'It seems to me that the use of the same term could be interpreted as a qualifier if used by females and an absolute if used by males.* For example:
"*Perhaps* you have misinterpreted me"
"*Maybe* you should do it again" '
(1980 p.35).

HEDGES

Quite a few studies have shown that in many situations, women do use more hedges than men do.

Fishman (1980), in the same research as above, found that **women used the hedge *you know* five times more than men.**

However, Lakoff's claim that hedges are directly linked with uncertainty and unassertiveness has been widely challenged. Fishman, for example, says that the hedges used in her study were another indicator that **the women were doing the conversational work:** the men were rejecting the topic of conversation and not responding, the women were attempting to keep the conversation going and get some kind of response.

Again, hedges, like tags, are used for more reasons, and more complicated reasons, than Lakoff suggested.

'SHE'S KIND OF FAT'

PERHAPS HE MISTOOK IT FOR HIS ONE'

IT'S SORTA LARGE'

'HE'S PROBABLY

YOU KNOW STRESSED

I MEAN, I THINK

IT SORT OF 'DEPENDS'

HYPERCORRECT GRAMMAR

Many researchers have found that women tend to use language more 'correctly' than men of the same social group. They are more likely to have standard English accents and grammar (see p.163-165) for how and why).

LASTLY, POLITENESS...

'Polite' is a very broad description of someone's behaviour and encompasses far more than saying 'please' and 'thank you'. One way of looking at the subject is Brown and Levison's (1978, 1987) model, which talks about 'face'. Politeness is respecting people's face wants which are:

1. **NEGATIVE FACE** – The need not to be imposed upon
2. **POSITIVE FACE** – The need to be liked and admired

So negative politeness includes all the things we do to avoid imposing our demands or point of view on others.

> **Like, if I knocked on your door and said 'Give me some sugar' that would be incredibly rude, you'd think it was a hold-up. But, if I said something like 'Sorry to bother you, I was just wondering if you had a few spoonfuls of sugar to spare. I've completely run out.',**

> **I would be respecting your negative face wants, by first of all apologising, and then by hedging the request and making it less direct. It gives you the option to refuse by admitting it's an imposition and adding things like 'to spare' which give you an easy way out: 'No sorry, I've just used all mine...'**

And positive politeness includes everything we might say to show that we agree with, respect and like someone...

> So if she were to start with a friendly greeting like 'Hi, how are you?' or a compliment: 'I was just admiring your garden, it looks great,' then she would also be using positive politeness by making you feel liked and admired.

> Some of the things we've already discussed do in fact relate to politeness:

NEGATIVE POLITENESS:

Using hedges or tags to soften a negative opinion or a demand.

POSITIVE POLITENESS:

Using affective tags to show support for another speaker. Asking questions to involve someone in the conversation.

It seems that Lakoff got this one right. **Women do seem to be more polite than men** and not just in the above ways. In the next section (co-operative v competitive conversation) we will discuss many ways in which women tend to support and encourage their conversational partners whilst men are more likely to dominate and pursue their own topics.

The crucial thing is that, as Janet Holmes puts it, *'The same linguistic devices can express different meanings in different contexts. There is nothing intrinsically polite about any linguistic form.'* (1995 p.10)

> **So although women do tend to be more polite than men, there are many other factors that affect not only how polite an individual is, but also what is considered polite. A few examples:**

<u>The norms of your social group</u> play an important role in determining what is polite. Amongst a group of young people using swear words and slang can express solidarity and friendliness and thus positive politeness, whereas the same vocabulary used when talking to your grandma could become very rude.

<u>How well you know someone</u> We tend to use more positive politeness with friends and more negative with strangers. While it shows positive politeness to call someone you know well by a nickname or term of endearment, to do the same to a stranger or distant acquaintance could be quite rude. On the other hand, to use negative politeness with a close friend can seem rude and distant.

<u>The formality of the situation</u> The same two people will use different levels of politeness in different situations. A teacher's son calls her 'mum' at home but 'Mrs Smith' in the classroom, two friends who are MPs use first names when down the pub but 'My Honourable Colleague' in Parliament.

<u>The status or power of the person you're talking to</u> We tend to use positive politeness more amongst equals and negative politeness when talking to superiors. So that, for example, a male employee might use far more negative politeness than his female employer when they talk. He might call her 'Mrs Parker' and apologise for bothering her when he wants to talk to her whilst she might use his first name and begin a conversation straight away with her question.

Finally, a look at the research of O'Barr and Atkins which attempts to redefine women's language.

POWERLESS LANGUAGE

O'Barr and Atkins (1980) analysed 150 hours of trials in a North Carolina courtroom looking at male and female witnesses' use of 'women's language' (features based on Lakoff). They found that

1. Women's Language was not used by all women
2. Although more women than men used it, its use wasn't restricted to women
3. The speaker's social status, and previous courtroom experience – not their sex – determined how many features of 'women's language' they would use (so a male ambulance driver with little courtroom experience uses far more W.L. features than a female pathologist who regularly appears in court).

So, they renamed it 'Powerless Language', suggesting that the reason it has been linked to women is that women in our society are normally less powerful than men.

So err...what can we conclude from all this then?

Well, perhaps that Lakoff and others may have put too much emphasis on individual features like tag questions and hedges, and not enough on their context.

And also that although it's difficult to draw up a list of features of women's language as Lakoff did, there are differences in the way women and men speak.

But the reasons for those differences are far more complicated than 'women being unsure of themselves and hesitant' and 'men being assertive'.

I thought we'd just established that it isn't sex but power that makes people use language differently.

Ah, well, not everyone agrees with O'Barr and Atkins. In fact, there are at least two studies that contradict their findings:

<u>Candace West</u> *(1984a; 1984b)* looked at doctor-patient conversations and found that doctors regularly interrupt their patients (which fits in with them being in the position of power), UNLESS the doctor is a woman and her patient a white man, in which case he will interrupt the doctor.
<u>Nicola Woods</u> *(1989)* recorded conversations between colleagues of different occupational status and found that even when the woman in the group was of the highest status, it was the man who dominated the conversation.

Denise O'Donoghue (Founder and Managing Director of Hat Trick Productions) commented that *'I see how men and women react differently in meetings. Men have sometimes totally misplaced my status... They have addressed themselves to a writer or a producer and I have been kind of talked over. I notice that the women I see on a daily basis change when they get into a meeting where there is a strong male contingent. I hear the anxiety in their voices, which is as much about needing to be heard as anything else. They have to keep going because they are still being talked over by men.'* (The Guardian p.2, 26 May 1997, 'Smashing the glass ceiling by Henry Porter')

So although status had some effect on language use, in their research it was sex that turned out to be a more important factor.

Things are never simple, are they?

Nope. What we probably ought to add to this is a look at

C♥MPETITIVE VERSUS CO-OPERATIVE CONVERSATION

These are words that have been used to describe the differences between women and men's use of language when in single sex groups.

They seem a bit vague. What exactly are they supposed to mean?

Well, its says here that 'Co-operativeness... refers to a particular type of conversation, where speakers work together to produce shared meanings. Set against this... is the notion of competitiveness: competitiveness is used to describe the adversarial style of conversation where speakers vie for turns and where participants are more likely to contradict each other than to build on each others' contributions.' (Coates p.118 in Cameron and Coates 1988)

AN OUTLINE OF SOME OF THE FEATURES OF CO-OPERATIVE CONVERSATION:

1. Speakers **build upon each other's comments,** so that topics of conversation are developed jointly and tend to shift gradually rather than abruptly from one to another.

2. Those not holding the floor 'listen actively'. That is, they
A **Use well-placed minimal responses** (*'uh-huh', 'umm', 'yeah'*) to show that they are listening and encourage the speaker to go on;
B **Interject questions and comments** into a speaker's turn without trying to interrupt and begin talking themselves;
C **May complete the speaker's utterance with or for them.**

3. Speakers are unlikely to disagree openly with other participants. They will use **hedges** to make their point less hard and fast. **Hedges** help statements to become negotiable and even retractable, depending on the rest of the group's comments.

4. Speakers will also use things like **hedges** and **tag questions** to respect the face needs of others when discussing sensitive issues.

5. **Tag questions** may be used in the middle of contributions to monitor whether others are in agreement.

This too, is taken from chapter 8 of Cameron and Coates 1988, in which Coates records the language of a group of women friends and analyses it for co-operative behaviour. She finds that they use all of these features and concludes:

'It seems that in conversations between women friends in an informal context, the notion of co-operativeness is not a myth' (p.119).

What seems to be lacking, though, is proof that men do the opposite.

That's true, in fact I'm sure not ALL men do, just like not ALL women will talk co-operatively. It's going to depend on loads of other factors like the size of the group, their social status, their relationship to each other...

Anyway, you're right, there isn't much research into all-men groups; what people mainly comment on is what happens in mixed-sex conversations, where the two styles meet: men dominate the conversation. Lets look at:

The silence of women in mixed-sex conversations

A popular myth is that women talk more than men. They gossip, natter, chatter, prattle, gibber, bicker and nag. In fact, research consistently contradicts this. It shows that **in mixed-sex conversations, men talk more.**

Spender suggests that the reason this myth exists is that we set different standards for men and women. Men's talk is valued and they have the right to talk, whereas women's talk is mere gossip and they are expected to remain silent in mixed-sex discussions. <u>So what 'women talk more' actually means is not that they talk more than men, but more than they ought to.</u>
(1980 pp.41-3)

HOW MEN END UP TALKING MORE

<u>Zimmerman and West (1975)</u> analysed single and mixed-sex conversations between two people, looking at **interruptions** and **overlaps** (which are both signs of breakdown in the 'rules' of conversational turntaking because they show one person cutting the other off mid-sentence or starting to speak before the other has finished.)

❤ They found that both sexes rarely interrupted or spoke over their conversational partners in the single sex pairs (<u>0.35 interruptions per conversation</u>), but that, in mixed sex pairs there were many more (<u>4.36 interruptions per conversation</u>)

❤ 98% of the interruptions and 100% of the overlaps were by the men.

❤ Men rarely interrupted or overlapped other men's speech, but they did both things a great deal to infringe upon a woman's right to speak.

❤ Conversely, women interrupted and overlapped men less than they did other women.

This suggests that men's dominance of conversation is a result of not just their behaviour, but women's too. Both sexes believe in men's dominance and right to speak more, so both sexes act in a way that encourages this.

So, the men interrupt a woman more than they would a man, but the women don't consider this out of order; in fact, they stop talking after being interrupted and they avoid interrupting the men.

The result of interruption: SILENCE

After being interrupted, people usually fall silent.

In 'an ideal conversation' there are very short silences as the conversation runs smoothly from one speaker to another.

Zimmerman and West also measured the silences that occurred in their conversations.

RESULTS:

Single-sex conversation: average silence = <u>1.35</u> seconds
Mixed-sex conversation: average silence = <u>3.21</u> seconds

As it was the women who kept being interrupted, it was the women who kept falling silent.
So, they spoke less than the men.

Minimal responses

Another reason for women's silence turned out to be **men delaying minimal responses.**
The women in Coates's study above made well-placed minimal responses to show that they were listening and supporting the speaker. The men in this study, however, made minimal responses, but they made them too late. Even a very short pause seems to change completely the function of the minimal response, so that it in fact indicates a lack of interest/support.
This lack of support often led the women to fall silent.

It seems to me that this idea of co-operativeness is a major step forward because it views 'Women's Language' in a positive light. It points out that although women may on average have less power than men, it doesn't mean their language is 'deficient', 'weak' or 'powerless'.

In fact, people's attitudes towards 'Women's Language' are beginning to change. People are (finally) comparing male and female speech with open minds. AND, surprise, surprise, finding that female speech isn't all bad.

There is now recognition that the co-operative style typically used by women is valuable for things like maintaining relationships, negotiating conflict and encouraging open discussion.

And so (dare I say it) it is more effective than the way men tend to speak in certain contexts.

West (1990) found that patients are more likely to co-operate with female doctors because of the way they use language.

Women used phrases like 'Okay, well let's make that our plan' or 'And then maybe you can stay away from the desserts...' compared to the men's: 'Lie down' or 'Take off your socks and shoes'.

But prejudice about the way we speak is only one of women's troubles because,

ENGLISH IS ANDROCENTRIC

HUH? ANDRO-WHAT?

Androcentric. It means it has a built-in bias towards men.

You mean it's sexist? But how can a language be sexist? Surely only the people who use it are sexist.

'Fraid not. For example: one researcher found that even though overall there are fewer words in the language relating to women than men, there are <u>220</u> English terms for a promiscuous female but only 20 for a male. (Stanley 1973)

So what? Doesn't mean the whole language is sexist.

Okay, how about this: almost all terms for women acquire derogatory meanings over time (if they didn't have them already), while most terms for men retain their original meanings or gain respect. Compare 'master' with 'mistress', 'Queen' with 'King', 'Madam' with 'Sir', 'Dame' with 'Earl', 'Lord', with 'Lady', and even 'man' with 'woman'. The terms for women have now either got negative connotations (often sexual) or lost the authority they once had, while the words for men retain their power and authority.

Did you know that in Roget's Thesaurus 'womanly' is listed under 'weakness' along with 'feebleness', 'debility' and 'impotence'?

Or that 'womanish' is listed under 'cowardice' with 'cry baby', 'quitter', 'spiritless' and 'craven'?

Whilst 'manliness' and 'manly' go with 'courage', 'moral fibre', 'resolution', 'heroism' and 'self-mastery'?

And another thing is that 'man' and 'he' are used to mean everyone, the whole race, even though half of us are female.

IN THIS ROOM WE HAVE THE WORK OF MANY OLD MASTERS AND MISTRESSES.

MY WHAT A MISTRESS PIECE !

> **Yeah but everyone knows that 'man' means woman as well, so what does it matter?**

> **That's just the point; we don't actually think of 'he/she' when we read 'man'. Our mental picture tends to exclude women.**

SOME EXAMPLES FROM REAL LIFE:

<u>Star Trek:</u> 'Our people are the best gamblers in the galaxy. We compete for power, fame, women.' *(People = men)**

<u>Elementary school textbook:</u> 'The brave pioneers crossed the plains with their wives, their children, and their cattle.' *(Pioneers = men)**

<u>Well-known riddle:</u> 'A man and his son are out fishing when the son has an accident. He is rushed to hospital, where a doctor is told to treat him, but the doctor gasps with horror and says: 'I can't treat the boy, he's my son!' How can this be? *(Doctor = man)**

<u>Hotel **advertisement**:</u> 'Anything any businessman or his wife would want' *(Businessman = man)**

> **Oh my God...**
> **You're not one of those PC fanatics are you? I bet you say 'person-hole-cover' and 'person-eating-tigers'**

* From Bolinger 1980 Longman

Well, yes, OK. Everyone knows that whole business has gone a bit too far. But it's easy to mock if you're a man – the language isn't biased against you. The sheer number of sexist words and phrases in the language is phenomenal…

EXAMPLES:
All the words that exclude women or are marked for women:

To suggest that a man is behaving like a woman is insulting, e.g.:

But, to use male terms for women is perceived as acceptable, and even complimentary, e.g.:

There are many words that mark women as men's property…

MANPOWER CHAIRMAN
LADY LAWYER
SCULPTRESS
FIREMAN
FEMALE DOCTOR
BIG GIRLS BLOUSE
OLD WOMAN
GIRLIE SPINSTER
TAKE IT LIKE A MAN
TOMBOY CHAPS
SPOKEN YOU GUYS
LIKE A MAN
MRS WIFE
WIDOW BAGGAGE

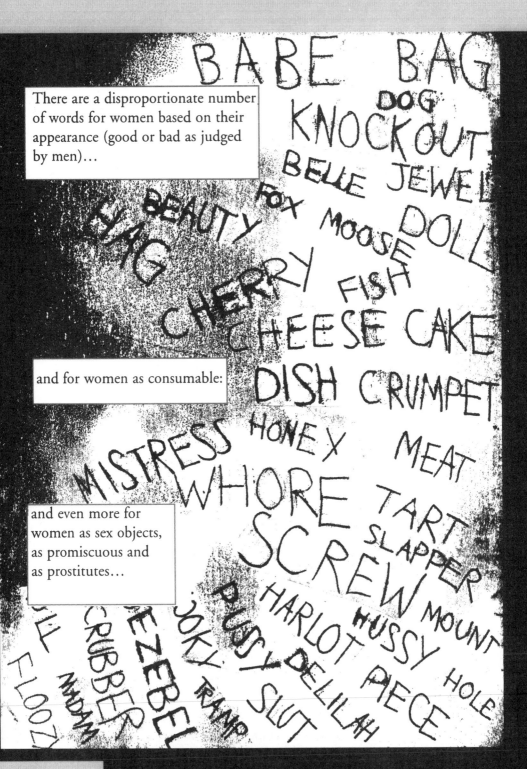

There are a disproportionate number of words for women based on their appearance (good or bad as judged by men)...

BABE BAG

DOG

KNOCKOUT

BELLE JEWEL

FOX

BEAUTY MOOSE DOLL

HAG CHERRY FISH

CHEESE CAKE

and for women as consumable:

DISH CRUMPET

MISTRESS HONEY MEAT

WHORE TART

and even more for women as sex objects, as promiscuous and as prostitutes...

SCREW SLAPPER

MOUNT

HARLOT HUSSY HOLE

SCRUBBER PUSSY PIECE

FLOOZY JEZEBEL TRAMP DELILAH

MADAM SLUT

OK, OK. Point made, but they're still just words. They can't hurt anyone.

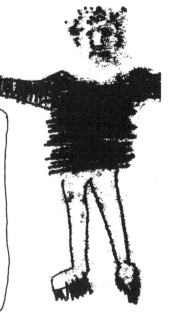

But they can. They're part of a whole culture's assumption that the male is the norm and that anything other is abnormal. So, words usually refer to the male unless marked (specified) otherwise. The marked term is nearly always the female, i.e.: 'doctor' and 'female doctor', 'manager' and 'manageress', 'host' and 'hostess'. The language perpetuates the attitude that a female doctor, host or manager is abnormal. The rare exceptions to this rule show and reinforce the old stereotypes and prejudices: you get 'secretaries' and 'male secretaries', 'nurses' and 'male nurses'.

All right! ALL RIGHT! Calm DOWN!

I am calm. I mean, it may seem petty to insist on the use of words like 'chairperson' and 'postal worker', but it's simply an attempt to even the score. Why should a woman who delivers letters be defined as female in her job title? What does her sex matter?

It's like women being either 'Miss' or 'Mrs' whilst men are just 'Mr'. We are defined by our relationship to men; even our names mark us as 'available' or 'taken'. Women even give up their names when they marry and take their husband's – their first name can even be replaced too, as in:

Mrs John P. Lowe
26 Manor Rd,
Kingsbury
Somerset.
TA 13 8 JK

Mr and Mrs J P. Lowe
26 Manor Road,
Kingsbury,
SOMERTON
Somerset
TA138JK

POSTPAK

Post Office

This not only labels women as property handed from father to husband; it also effectively eliminates women from history.

As Virginia Woolf said in 1972 (p.41), '*The history of England is the history of the male line*'. Very little is known of women's role.

Many women are now keeping their name when they marry, or going further and avoiding their father's name too, by coining new names for themselves, often using their mother's given name as a surname.

The language we have inherited has been built by men, and represents men's point of view. This is why there are loads of terms for attractive and indeed ugly women (as sex-objects appreciated/scorned by men) but very few specific to men. And why women are labelled for the convenience of men as 'another man's property' or 'up for grabs'.

Oh now hang on a minute. This is going too far. How can language have been 'built by men'? Women have been around and talking for just as long as men have.

How and why English has been built by Men*

'Historically, women have been excluded from the production of cultural forms, and language is, after all, a cultural form... In fairly crude terms this means that language has been built by men and that they have used it for their own purposes.' [Spender 1980 p.52]

It is obvious (but easy to forget) that language was not just 'there' to be picked up and used by humans; our names for things are not natural – we created them. The origins of contemporary English are fantastically complicated and we can't go right back to the beginning and plot the whole development. What we can do is look at how it is now, at the trends and biases, and then work backwards, and look at why.

As we have shown, contemporary English has a built-in bias towards men. The reason has a lot to do with its being built by them:

The truth is that throughout history both women and men have created meanings to classify their experience of the world. **BUT**, the language we've got now represents almost entirely men's experience, **because** historically, women just haven't been **THE PEOPLE WITH THE POWER**. They haven't been in a position to get their meanings heard and worked into the language. They weren't educated and they weren't the influential politicians, teachers, philosophers, public speakers, writers or linguists. And so, any meanings that they used weren't influential; they were cut off from the main stream and more often than not, have been lost.

* Source: Spender 1980

Having the power also means to be the ones who legislate and lay down the rules. Here *(just to make absolutely clear that 'insignificant' things like the use of 'man' and 'he' as generic terms did not arise by chance)* are a few examples of male writing and rule-making on the subject:

- 1553 – A Mr Wilson decreed that it was more natural for the man to come before the woman (as in *'male and female'*, *'Mr and Mrs'*, *'brother and sister'*)
- 1746 – John Kirkby wrote *Eighty Grammatical Rules*. Rule 21 said that the male gender was *'more comprehensive'* than the female
- 1850 – an Act of Parliament was passed stating that *'he'* should be used for both sexes

Note that these men were addressing an almost entirely male audience – women were not educated, and there were no female members of Parliament. So who was to question men's *'comprehensiveness'* or their *'naturally'* coming first?

In Summary: language was built by men because society was controlled by men, and it is **The People with the Power** in society who can build their reality, their point of view, into the language.

Well, you've convinced me. Language is prejudiced against women. But what can...

Wait a second. Women aren't the only ones who get a raw deal. English isn't simply a male point of view – it's a WHITE male point of view.

white adj. **1.** snow-white, snowy, chalk-white, chalky, ivory, creamy, milky, milk-white, oyster-white, off white; silver, hoary: *Many building in the tropics are painted white. Do you believe that a person's hair can turn white overnight?* **2.** pale, pallid, pasty, wan, whey-faced, ashen, bloodless drained whitish, waxen, ghastly, ghostly, anaemic, dead white, deathly white, cadaverous, corpse-like: *Her black dress contrasted starkly with her white complexion.* **3.** innocent pure, unsullied, stainless, unblemished, spotless, immaculate, virginal, virtuous, undefiled, chaste: *She came to you with white hands, which you have sought to dirty with your vicious accusations.* **4.** Caucasian, Cascasoid, light skinned, fair-skinned, pale-complexioned: *The American Indian was – and still is – treated very unfairly by the White man.*

AS you can see, there are **some** negative synonyms for *white,* but not **nearly** as many as for *black.*

black *adj.* **1.** jet, jet-black, coal-black, inky, sooty, swart, swarthy, raven, ebony, dusky, *Literary* ebon, hyacinthine: *Her hair was as black as coal.* **2.** Negro, Negroid, dark skinned, *often offensive* coloured: *Most of the Black races originated near or south of the equator.* **3.** dark, pitch-black, jet-black, coal black, Stygian; starless, moonless: *He bundled his coat round himself and walked into the black night.* **4.** dark, sombre, dusky, gloomy, menacing, glowering louringor lowering, threatening, funeral: *The sky became black with storm clouds.* **5.** malignant, baleful, baneful, deadly, deathly, sinister, dismal, hateful, disastrous: *It was a black day when he came into my life.* **6.** bad, foul, iniquitous, wicked, evil, diabolic(al), infernal, hellish, atrocious, awful, malicious, abominable, outrageous, vicious, villaineous, flagitious, vile, disgraceful, unscrupolous, unconscionable, unprincipled, blackguardly, knavish, perfidious, insidious, nefarious, dastardly, treacherous, unspeakable, shameful, scurvy, criminal, felonious: *You have told the blackest lies about me.* **7.** angry, wrathful, furious, frowning, bad tempered, sulky, resentful, clouded, threatening, glowering: *She gave him a black look and he withered in abject fear.* -v. **8.** boycott, embargo, blacklist, ban, interdict: Because of the dispute over plumbers' wages, the other building-trades unionshave blacked every manufacturer in the business.

And what about all the negative phrases with 'black' in:

BLACKLEG
BLACKLIST
BLACK LOOKS
THE BLACK ART
BLACKBALLED
BLACK MAGIC
BLACK IN THE FACE
BLACKMAIL
BLACK FRIDAY
THE BLACK DEATH
THE BLACK SHEEP OF THE FAMILY
BLACK IN SOMEONE'S
TO BE IN BLACK WASHING
THE BLACK-A-MOOR WHITE
BLACK BOOKS
BLACK MASS
BLACK HEARTED
BLACK DOG
BLACK SPOT
BLACK GUARDS

The writer James Baldwin described his feelings on the subject:
'For a black writer in this country to be born into the English language, is to realise that the assumptions on which the language operates are his enemy... I was forced to reconsider similes: as black as sin, as black as night, black hearted.'
(*Los Angeles Times* 1979)

Well, I can see how degrading it must be to be surrounded by all these anti-black metaphors but we can take some consolation from the fact that most of these terms stem from non-racist roots.

That's true

SOME WORD HISTORIES (ETYMOLOGIES)

'**BLACK DEATH**' – from the dark spots that appeared on the skin of plague sufferers.

'**BLACK MAGIC**' – Coined because a scribe accidentally copied the Greek word 'necromanteia' (magic involving summoning the spirits of the dead from the underworld) as 'nigromantia', which was then interpreted as coming from the Latin for black ('nigro') and translated into English as such in the Middle Ages.

'**TO BLACKEN SOMEONE'S CHARACTER**' – comes from the Anglo-Saxon verb 'blaekan' (to scorch or burn).

Many of the words/phrases linking 'black' with unpleasantness and evil stem from an understandable fear of the dark and night before artificial light. The same associations are to be found in many other languages including Swahili and other African languages.

(Source: Linda Hall in Palmer 1986)

You're right, those phrases, don't originate in racism, but what about the number of insulting words used specifically to describe us:

Derogatory names for people of colour used by white people (now or in the past):

Terms specific to black women:

Those for black children:

And those relating to black people as workers/slaves:

And these are just a selection.

SAMBO
NIGGER
BLACKY INKFACE
HOTTENTOT
JIGABOO GOLLYWOG MUDFACE
BLACKAMUFFIN
SADE
SMUTTBUTT SHITSKIN
BLACKDOLL
NIGGER-GIRL BLACK SKIRT
BLACK SCUTTLE-SAULT SEAL
BLACK DIAMOND MAMA
TAR BABY SPADELET
NIGGERKIN
NIGGERLING NIGGERTAR-BABY
BLACK IVORY
BOY COOLIE
BLACK LAUNDRY QUEEN
BOAT NIGGER BLACK BIRDS

(Source: Green 1996)

Yes there is an inordinate number of abusive terms for black people. Once you start to look at derogatory language though, you find out just how suspicious all cultures are of racial or religious difference. There are startling numbers of insulting labels for all nationalities. Take a look at the reverse side of the coin – black people's names for whites:

White women:

Whites and their skin colour (washed out black):

Whites as oppressors:

Whites as ignorant peasants

LADY SNOW PALE SAULT
SNOW BUNNY
GREY BROAD WHITE EYES
PINK TOES WHITE MEAT
GREY BALE OF STRAW
GREY SKIN
SNOWBALL PALE ANAMIC PALEFACE
WIGGER FACE NIGGER
PINK WHOOGIE
CHUCK
HACK HOOPLE PIGS MR GUB
CHARLIE
PLAIN FOLKS WOODHICK
PECKERWOOD
CRACKER CAVEBOY

(Source: Green 1996)

OK! OK! OK! CALM DOWN EVERYBODY! So now you see where PC language came from.

Yeah, right... But what they're saying is that language represents the point of view of someone who's a white, straight, middle-aged, able-bodied, male, who's not ugly or fat or too skinny; who's of average height and intelligence and hasn't got wonky teeth, or glasses.

I mean... Who IS this GUY? I don't think I've ever met anybody like this!

No, me neither. It's just part of human nature to pick on people who are different or weaker than you are.

SOME EXAMPLES:

Illness, the Oxford Thesaurus lists the following words under 'ill': *'bad, wicked, sinful, evil, iniquitous, immoral, depraved, vicious, vile, wrong, corrupt'* and for **'sick'** it lists: *'peculiar, unconventional, strange, weird, odd, bizarre, grotesque, macabre, shocking, ghoulish, morbid, gruesome, stomach turning, sadistic, masochistic, sado-masochistic'*

When it comes to **disability**, we find: *'impairment, defect, incapacity, unfitness, impotence, powerlessness, helplessness, crippled, lame, damaged, ruined, harmed, non-functioning',* and so on.

The Poor are labelled with a term that also means *'low, bad, skimpy, inadequate, deficient, insufficient, sparse, awful, rotten, lousy, unsatisfactory'*

The linguist Dwight Bolinger sums up the situation like this: *'When Moses said to the children of Israel... 'Thou shalt not curse the deaf, nor put a stumbling block before the blind' (Leviticus 19,14) he was countering what seems to be a universal flaw in human nature: to build self-esteem by looking down on those less fortunate.'* (p.89)

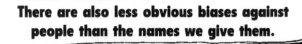

There are also less obvious biases against people than the names we give them.

'TOMORROW I'M GOING TO REWRITE THE ENGLISH LANGUAGE.'
BY LOIS KEITH

Tomorrow I am going to rewrite the English Language.
I will discard all those striving ambulist metaphors
of power and success
And construct new ways to describe my strength.
My new, different strength.

Then I won't have to feel dependent
Because I can't stand on my own two feet.
And I'll refuse to feel a failure
When I don't stay one step ahead.
I won't feel inadequate if I can't
Stand up for myself
Or illogical when I don't
Take it one step at a time.

I will make them understand that it is a very male way
To describe the world.
All this walking tall
And making great strides.

Yes, tomorrow I am going to rewrite the English Language.
Creating the world in my own image.
Mine will be a gentler, more womanly way
To describe my progress.
I will wheel, cover and encircle.
Somehow I will learn to say it all.
(Ed. Keith 1994 p.57)

So, the whole language is prejudiced against everyone!

Well yes, in a way... but to varying degrees. It has to be said that the gender bias is far more deeply rooted in the structure of the language than many of these other issues. However, they are all right; there's just no such thing as neutral language.

This is terrible! How can we change language for the better?

Well, it's very difficult to change things, as past attempts show: 'Ms', for example, was a new term, intended as a parallel to 'Mr' (a title that doesn't mark you as married/single) but it has turned into yet another negatively marked term for a woman. It's associated with feminists, business women, widows or those who are seen as having some sort or grudge against men.

Oh dear!

And the 'he/she' case is another good example. Lots of people have tried creating new neutral pronouns to get round the problem, but how do you actually get people to use them? Its just like PC language: anything new is good for a laugh.

Here are some of the suggestions for how to replace the supposedly neutral pronoun 'he' in sentences like:

*'If the customer has any complaints **he** should address them to the management.'*

*'If the customer has any complaints **she, he/she, heshe, thon, on, co, E, et, heesh, hesh, hir, hirm, hizer, ho, jhe, mon, na, ne, per, po, tey, xe** should address them to the management.'*

In this book we have chosen to alternate the pronouns *'he'* and *'she'*, although in common usage (especially spoken language) *'they'* is increasingly used. This use of plural for singular is frowned on by many linguists but it is interesting that this form was in fact the common usage before the 19th-century prescriptive grammarians 'corrected' grammar with their rule books and Acts of Parliament. (Source: Crystal 1995)

New terms are always being invented for disability, too. But each new term tends to gain negative connotations because able-bodied people are still prejudiced. Why else would an organisation to support cerebral palsy sufferers change its name from 'The Spastics Society' to 'SCOPE'?

THAT'S right. I read about something like that in Ben Elton's novel Gridlock.

There is a debate surrounding the word 'spastic'. This concerns its appropriation by those who do not suffer from cerebral palsy, as a term of contempt. There can scarcely be any able-bodied person who has not used, or at least failed to confront the use of the word 'spastic' as an insult. It is normally a youthful insult, particularly beloved of small, farty boys ('Cripes spew face, you're such a spastic'), but it resonates throughout the population. We all know that to call someone a 'spastic' means that they are stupid, worthless and beneath contempt. Hence the debate for those who actually are spastics about what to do with such a tainted term. It's their word, it describes a condition from which they suffer, but it has been stolen, and the question is, do they want it back? Since the word spastic has come to imply an all-encompassing and extremely negative summation of a person's

abilities and personality, is the word any longer of any real relevance to those who suffer from cerebral palsy? Has the very word itself not become yet another cross that people with this condition are fated to bear? Some say yes, some say that the word has been debased beyond redemption. Some say that it must be discarded as a lost cause, and that a new, untained word or phrase must be found. They suggest 'C.P. sufferer' for instance, a phrase which certainly has the advantage of clearly only describing an aspect of a person, and not appearing to sum up their entire personality. On the other hand, there are those who insist that the word 'spastic' must be reclaimed. It must be wrested from the mouths of thoughtless little boys and restored to its true meaning. These people look to a day when they will be able to say 'I am a spastic' without it sounding a bit like a gag.

Ben Elton, *Gridlock*, 1991, p.22

These examples show that the problem goes deeper than individual words or grammatical rules. Abolishing prejudiced language (if it were possible) wouldn't get rid of prejudiced attitudes.

And creating new positive words won't solve the problem either because it's not the word itself that's racist, sexist or whatever, it's the meaning we give it.

So, new, supposedly neutral words for stigmatised groups gradually acquire negative meanings because society is still prejudiced against the people being described.

The bad news is that while the bias in language still exists, it actually makes the situation worse. If the word for a person 'suffering from congenital paralysis due to some cerebral lesion or impairment' ('a spastic') is also used to mean someone who is stupid and worthless, the word is bound to prejudice speakers against CP sufferers.

Dale Spender points out that we should look deeper than individual words because:
'the problem lies not in the words but in the semantic rule which governs their positive or negative connotations' (1980, p.29)

The *'semantic rule'* she is discussing goes like this: **words which refer to women occupy a *'negative semantic space'* so that they acquire a pejorative (negative) meaning.**
THIS MEANS THAT TO ABOLISH SEXIST WORDS WE WOULD HAVE TO ABOLISH VIRTUALLY ALL WORDS ABOUT WOMEN, **AND** IT WOULDN'T HELP ANYWAY because the semantic rule would still exist so that any new words replacing the abolished ones would themselves become negative.

Also, words that are not seen as inherently sexist would still represent a bias. The word 'aggressive', for example, has very different connotations when applied to women as opposed to men.

P♥WER & LANGUAGE

Here are the theories; see what you think.

1. THOUGHT IS GOVERNED BY LANGUAGE.

This is often called *'The Sapir-Whorf Hypothesis'*, because around the beginning of the 20th century Edward Sapir (1884-1939) and Benjamin Lee Whorf (1897-1941) put forward the theory that our language determines the way we think ('linguistic determinism') and that, because of this, different languages make their speakers think differently.

For proof, they looked for **the differences between languages.**
One of the languages that Whorf studied was the Amerindian language, **Hopi.**
Here are some of the ways in which it differs from English:

VOCABULARY: It has just one word for everything that flies except birds (insects, aeroplanes, pilots...).

GRAMMAR: Compared to English, Hopi is a 'timeless language'. It does not differentiate between past, present and future. English treats 'time' as objective: it is accurate and measurable, it has solid divisions between the past, present and future. The Hopi Indians talk about time only subjectively: as it appears to the speaker. For example, they say, *'I left on the third day'* instead of our, *'I left after three days'*.

♥ They have no words or grammatical forms that refer directly to time, whilst we have a great number: *'early', 'late', 'on time', 'punctual'*.

♥ Another way in which we mark time is with verb tenses. So that the verb *'to be'* becomes:

| *Past tense:* **'I was'** | *Present tense :* **'I am'** | *Future tense:* **'I will be'** |

Hopi doesn't use these, either. Instead it has different verb endings to show how certain the speaker is about an event (e.g., whether she saw something happen herself or whether she's just heard about it) and different voice inflections to show whether the person talking is reporting an event, expecting an event or generalising about events.

Sapir and Whorf claimed that it would be virtually impossible for an English scientist and a Hopi to understand each other's thinking, because their languages, which are their way of dividing up and ordering the world, differ so much.

Well, it sounds quite convincing but, when you think about it, you can always translate one language into another. Even if the outcome ends up clumsy and long-winded, it can be understood. How would that be possible if concepts were unique to the speakers of a particular language?

That's true, the very fact that the conceptual differences of Hopi can be explained in English is a pretty solid argument against the theory.

Yes and another is that the speakers of one language can grasp a concept invented by those of another, even if they don't have words for it. So, the fact that Australian aboriginal languages often have few words for numbers, doesn't stop them using western arithmetic as well as any English person if taught.

And what about thinking without language? Lots of 'Creative Thinkers', like Einstein, Micheal Faraday and S.T. Coleridge insisted that their inspirations came as mental images, not words.

Um, and, we all visualise and think about things like paintings, maps, music, and what someone looks like without using language.

Yeah, and everybody gets that feeling sometimes where you just can't find the words to convey what you're thinking. If language governed our thoughts, then how could we possibly think about things that we can't find words for?

We wouldn't be able to, just like we wouldn't be able to invent new words. Language change wouldn't exist if the Sapir-Whorf theory were right.

So, um... are you two now arguing that language doesn't affect our thoughts <u>at all</u>, because...

No, no, there is more support for what is known as the 'weak version' of the Sapir-Whorf hypothesis.

THE WEAK VERSION:

This suggests that although language does not **determine** what we can think about, it does **affect** our thinking on some level.

For example, there is evidence to suggest that language can have a powerful effect on our memories. In an experiment by **Carmichael, Hogan and Walter (1932)**, two groups of people were shown simple pictures, then asked to remember and redraw them. Each group was given a different name for the picture. They found that the drawing's name had quite an effect on people's memory of it.

Here are some examples:

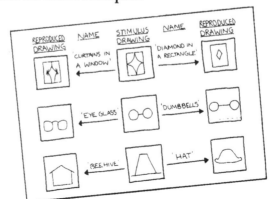

EYE WITNESS TESTIMONY:

Elizabeth Loftus has conducted lots of research into the reliability of EYEWITNESS TESTIMONY. She gets people to watch videos of accidents and then fill in a questionnaire; different groups are asked slightly different questions, and their responses are compared:

QUESTION:	AVERAGE ANSWER:
*'About how fast were the cars going when they **contacted**?'*	*31.8 m.p.h.*
*'About how fast were the cars going when they **hit**?"*	*34.0 m.p.h.*
*'About how fast were the cars going when they **bumped**?"*	*38.1 m.p.h.*
*'About how fast were the cars going when they **collided**?"*	*39.3 m.p.h.*
*'About how fast were the cars going when they **smashed**?"*	*40.8 m.p.h.*

(Loftus and Palmer 1974)

As you can see, the connotations of a single word can alter people's recollection.

The really interesting part is that a week later, Loftus retested some of the same people (without reshowing the video) to see whether these questions had truly affected their memories, or just their account on that day.

She asked three groups of people whether they had seen any broken glass:

Group	Percentage who remembered seeing the (non existent) glass
Those who had been asked a 'smashed' question:	32
Those who had been asked a 'hit' question:	14
And another group who hadn't been asked about speed:	12

These experiments suggest that although language doesn't actually **govern** thought, it can **distort** at least one area of thought: our memories.

Many linguists agree that although it isn't feasible to claim that language determines thought, it is likely that:

'Language plays an active and crucial – If qualified – role in shaping (though not completely determining) the processes of representation, by "pointing us towards different types of observation" and "predisposing certain choices of interpretation".'

(Montgomery 1986 p.175)

Or that

'The influence of language on thought is indisputable but it is not as absolutely determining as Whorf has argued.'

(Anderson 1988 p.83)

So what we're saying is that the degree to which language affects thoughts depends partly on your definition of thought: is it just conscious 'thinking' or do you go with a much wider definition that includes memory, perception, emotions, problem solving and so on?

As always, there is of course an alternative argument:

2. LANGUAGE IS GOVERNED BY THOUGHT.

The opposite argument to Whorf's is the 'Universalist view'. It proposes that humans, wherever they're from, think in similar ways: our common inheritance means that we all have the same set of basic concepts: **'conceptual primes'**.

And because we think similarly, our languages will all have some means of expressing these conceptual primes (the basic, important things).

Like:	*relative height:*	*relative distance:*	*and relative time:*
	UP DOWN	NEAR FAR	THEN NOW

Since the 1950s and Chomsky's Generative Grammer (see page 40) the focus has changed and linguists have been looking for **simularities between languages**, rather than differences. There is great interest in the idea of '**Language Universals**' (common features between the world's languages), like:

❤ *All languages have something very similar to our nouns and verbs.*

Although, it has so far proved very difficult actually to identify many universals that apply to all languages without exception, many trends and patterns of similarity have been found.

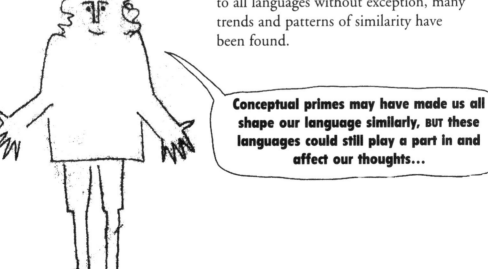

Conceptual primes may have made us all shape our language similarly, BUT these languages could still play a part in and affect our thoughts...

Many linguists now believe that <u>thought and language are interdependent</u>: although the two are separate and can function alone, language often facilitates thought, and we have to think to understand and use language.

Yes, that idea is backed up by the fact that we sometimes talk to ourselves and 'think out loud': language is aiding our thought processes. It's like how the act of explaining something to someone else often helps you to understand it better yourself.

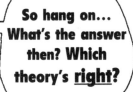

So hang on... What's the answer then? Which theory's <u>right</u>?

Well, as you can see, it's difficult to say for sure, but it seems that the extreme end of either theory is a bit unlikely: language doesn't rule thought, but we can't claim that it has absolutely no effect on it.

...put it this way; I'm convinced
...nguage has some control over
...r thoughts, because it's so
...ul. You just have to look at the
...nguage is used to manipulate:

...about the sway a great public
...r can have over her audience,
for example:

ORATORY or RHETORIC *(The art of persuasive speaking/writing)*

There are many techniques that are used by public speakers to interest their audience and make their argument convincing. **Max Atkinson** (1984), who has studied these devices in depth, calls them '**CLAPTRAPS**', because speakers use them to get the audience participating by clapping, cheering, booing, etc. **The most effective claptraps he identified are:**

§ <u>Lists of three</u>: '*The past with its crimes, its follies, and its tragedies…*' *
'*These cruel, wanton, indiscriminate bombings.*' * '*Killing large numbers of civilians, and women and children*' *

§ <u>Contrastive pairs</u> : '*You do your worst, and we will do our best*'… *

§ <u>Positive Evaluation of us</u> : '*The people of this mighty imperial city…*' *
'*Little does he know the spirit of the British nation, or the tough fibres of the Londoners*' *

§ <u>Negative evaluation of them</u>: *The Nazi war machine with its clanking, heel-clicking, dandified Prussian officers, its crafty expert agents fresh from the cowing and tying down of a dozen countries… the dull, drilled, docile, brutish masses of the Hun soldiery.* *

But there are literally hundreds of other devices, many of which have been used, written about and studied since classical times. Although they may not all draw applause, they do contribute to making the speaker more believable, authoritative and persuasive. They make a speech/piece of writing more powerful.

| Here's a small selection: |

§ *Repetition of words for effect:* 'We shall fight him by land, we shall fight him by sea, we shall fight him in the air.' *
'The Russian danger is therefore our danger, and the danger of the United States, just as the cause of any Russian fighting for his hearth and home is the cause of free men and free peoples in every quarter of the globe' *

§ *Alliteration:* 'The dull, drilled, docile, brutish masses of the Hun soldiery *
'We will mete out to the Germans the measure, and more than the measure, that they have meted out to us *

§ *Onomatopoeia:* 'the Nazi war machine with its clanking, heel-clicking, dandified Prussian officers' *

§ *Metaphor:* 'What he has done is to kindle a fire in British hearts, here and all over the world... He has lighted a fire which will burn with a steady and consuming flame until the last vestiges of Nazi tyranny have been burnt out of Europe' ❖

§ *Simile:* 'The Hun soldiery plodding on like a swarm of crawling locusts' *

§ *Highly emotive language:* 'German troops violated the frontiers' *
'He hopes... that he will terrorise and cow the people of this mighty imperial city.' ❖

§ *Rhetorical questions:* 'You ask, what is our policy? I will say: it is to wage war, by sea, land and air.' ✳ 'You ask, what is our aim? I can answer in one word: it is victory...' ✳

§ *Use of negatives and double negatives:* 'From this nothing will turn us – nothing. We will never parley, we will never negotiate with Hitler or any of his gang.' * 'We ask no favours of the Enemy. We seek from them no compunction.' *

All extracts taken from speeches by Winston Churchill:
* BBC broadcast, 22 June 1941   ❖ BBC broadcast, 11 September 1940
✱ BBC broadcast, 27 April 1941   ✳ 13 May 1940 (from Hansard, 5th series, issue no.1096)

The language used in advertising is notoriously persuasive. By using words along with music and visuals, advertisers attempt (and often manage) to sell people products that they would not otherwise buy. That's power.

Some commonly used words:

Euphemisms:

'fun size'/'regular'	=	small*
'crafted'	=	manufactured*
'farm fresh' (eggs)	=	battery farmed
'budget'/'value'	=	cheap
'man-made'/'costume'	=	fake*

* From Bolinger 1980

The product is: *the first, the biggest, the best, the latest, the finest, the smoothest, the most powerful, lighter, faster, better, authentic, rustic, vintage, original, traditional, classic, genuine, quality, style, luxury, superb, magnificent, beautiful, outstanding, special, exclusive, distinctive, unique, ultimate, exceptional, advanced, refined, sophisticated, perfect, recommended, award winning, new, revolutionary, innovative, state-of-the-art, carefully selected and value for money.*

The producers are: *the people who care, experienced, precise, expert, craftsmen, creators, designers, specialists, engineers, professional, number one, leading, major, world wide, confident, trusted, innovative and reliable.*
They have: *expertise, knowledge, skills, long-term commitment, inspiration, authority and international recognition.*

Euphemisms like those above are words that present their (unpleasant) subject in a favourable light.

EUPHEMISMS and DYSPHEMISMS (their opposite) are used all the time by the media, politicians and other people in power to manipulate the way they present information.

HERE ARE A FEW EXAMPLES:

EUPHEMISM	DYSPHEMISM
freedom-fighter	terrorist
casualties	dead bodies*
tragedy	crime*
public relations	propaganda*
to let go	to sack
care in the community	abandonment

AND SOME MILITARY EUPHEMISMS:

(* Bolinger 1980
pp.115-119)
(✷ Montgomery
1986 p.179)

mission	bombing raid*
collateral damage	killing the civilian population✷
demographic targeting	killing the civilian population✷
a pre-emptive strike	getting your retaliation in first✷
enhanced radiation weapon	neutron bomb (destroys people not property)✷

As the eyewitness-testimony research shows, this kind of language can affect not only our perception, but also our memory of events.

A sinister example of words being used to mask reality is the language the Nazis used:

WORDS AS WEAPONS

In the 1930s and '40s, the Nazis used a system of linguistic camoufla (euphemism). Here are some examples of the terminology their 'Language-rules' dictated*:

'The Final Solution of the Jewish problem'	=	the extinction of German Jewry through death camps.
'Evacuation'	=	removal of enemies to slavery and death
'Special Treatment'	=	death (usually by gas)
'Protective Custody'	=	imprisonment in concentration camp

This linguistic disguise helped the Nazis to carry out the atrocities of the holocaust – both on an international and on an individual level.

It was far easier to give the order for thirty people to receive *special treatment* than to command the execution by gas of those people. Especially if the people who were on the receiving end had been reduced to the status of *vermin* by the authority that gave you *your* orders.

The language used also made it easier for the rest of the world to ignore what was going on, until it was too late.

(Source: Justman 1995 pp. 90-1)

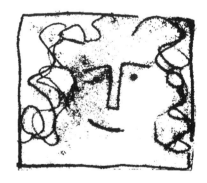

Those examples are particularly obvious euphemisms, but euphemisms are everywhere. They appear most in areas that society considers difficult or taboo, like death, bodily functions and sex.

Yes, because words for 'difficult subjects' become tainted by being associated with that subject, and so are replaced by a 'nicer' word which becomes tainted by its association and is replaced by a 'nicer' word which becomes...

As we use euphemisms to cover up areas of discomfort, they show up exactly what we as a society 'don't like to talk about'.

Robin Lakoff (1975), suggests that 'lady' has become a euphemism for woman: *'it is discouraging to note that at least one euphemism for "woman" does exist and is very much alive. The word of course is 'lady'.* She continues, *'Just as we do not call whites "Caucasian-Americans", there is no felt need to refer to men commonly as "gentlemen". And just as there is a felt need for such terms as "Afro-Americans", there is similarly a felt need for "lady".'* (1975 pp.20-1)

Others too, claim that the continually changing names for minority groups are euphemisms: *'The revolving cycle of euphemism has turned full circle in the United States: black has become acceptable, replacing Afro-American, which replaced Negro, which replaced coloured, which replaced darky, which in turn replaced black.'* (Howard 1977)

AN EXCERPT FROM... 'ON BEING A CRIPPLE' – NANCY MAIRS

First, the matter of semantics. I am a cripple. I chose this word to name me. I chose from among several possibilities, the most common of which are *handicapped* and *disabled*. I made the choice a number of years ago, without thinking, unaware of my motives for doing so. Even now, I'm not sure what those motives are, but I recognise that they are complex and not entirely flattering. People – crippled or not – wince at the word *cripple*, as they do not at the word *handicapped* or *disabled*. Perhaps I want them to wince. I want them to see me as a tough customer, one to whom the fates/gods/viruses have not been kind, but who can face the brutal truth of her existence squarely. As a cripple I swagger. But, to be fair to myself, a certain amount of honesty underlies my choice. *Cripple* seems to me a clean word, straightforward and precise. It has an honourable history, having made its first appearance in the Lindisfarne Gospel in the tenth century. As a lover of words, I like the accuracy with which it describes my condition: I have lost the full use of my limbs. *Disabled*, by contrast, suggests any incapacity, physical or mental. And I certainly don't like *handicapped*, which implies that I have deliberately been put at a disadvantage, by whom I cannot imagine (my God is not a Handicapper General) in order to increase chances in the great race of life. These words seem to me to be moving away from my position, to be widening the gap between word and reality. Most remote is the recently coined euphemism *differently abled*, which partakes of the same semantic hopefulness that transformed countries from *undeveloped* to *underdeveloped*, and then to *less-developed* and finally to *developing* nations. People have continued to starve in those countries during the shift. Some realities do not obey the dictates of language. (Ed. Saxton and Howe 1988 p.119)

As Nancy Mairs points out, there is a danger that euphemisms and PC language go so far to avoid abuse/discrimination that they become inaccurate: what is language for if not to discriminate between things?

You're right, we can't pretend that blacks and whites aren't different colours, or that calling things like poor, exploited countries by a different name will actually improve the situation there.

No, sorting out prejudice in language should never be considered as separate from the problem in the real world.

So, to sort things out we need to tackle both at once? Language and society?

Yes, it sounds difficult and in truth, it is. These things do take time, but the process has already started. Attempts to change language, even if not accepted, raise people's awareness of the bias and make people think about what they say, and the gradual improvements in society make it easier for language change to be accepted.

chapter Four:

VARIETY AND CHANGE

Part 1

LANGUAGE VARIETIES pg. 146

☎ How does the language we use vary according to who we are and where we come from?

Part 2

LANGUAGE CHANGE pg. 169

☎ Is language change good or bad?

☎ Where do new words, sounds and grammatical structures come from and how do

☎ they spread?

What will happen to English in the future?

PART ONE:

lANGUage VaRietieS

There are around **320 MILLION PEOPLE**
worldwide whose first language is English.
It is about 450 million people's
second language, and there are roughly
a billion people who understand it.
(*The Sunday Times* Word Power Supplement 1993 part 3)

English is without a doubt a global language. However, these phenomenal numbers of people do not all speak an identical, invariant, unchanging language. Every language is a composite of many different dialects and the farther it spreads, the more this is true.

THERE ARE MILLIONS OF VARIETIES OF GLOBAL ENGLISH:

GLOBAL ENGLISH

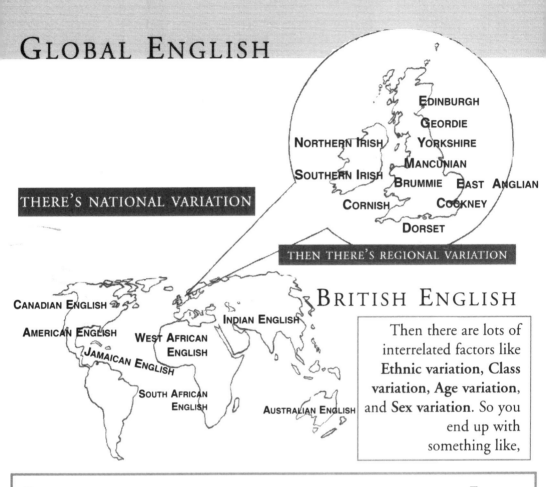

THERE'S NATIONAL VARIATION

EDINBURGH
GEORDIE
YORKSHIRE
NORTHERN IRISH
MANCUNIAN
SOUTHERN IRISH
BRUMMIE   EAST ANGLIAN
CORNISH   COCKNEY
DORSET

THEN THERE'S REGIONAL VARIATION

CANADIAN ENGLISH
AMERICAN ENGLISH   WEST AFRICAN ENGLISH
JAMAICAN ENGLISH
INDIAN ENGLISH
SOUTH AFRICAN ENGLISH
AUSTRALIAN ENGLISH

BRITISH ENGLISH

Then there are lots of interrelated factors like **Ethnic variation, Class variation, Age variation,** and **Sex variation.** So you end up with something like,

BRITISH, YORKSHIRE, WHITE, MIDDLE-CLASS, MIDDLE-AGED, FEMALE ENGLISH

and even that will vary according to things like the formality of the situation and the individual: no two people use language in the same way; we all have our own 'IDIOLECT' – our own quality and tones of voice, habitual vocabulary, frequently used phrases, ways of arguing a point, and so on.

Hello, do you speak my personal variety of British, Yorkshire, white, middle-class, middle-aged, female English?

The differences between varieties of English can be extreme or slight. They can be phonological, semantic, grammatical, pragmatic or all of these. Differences are usually far more apparent in speech than in writing, where there is more of a standard.

What is standard English?

It was once a dialect of English like any other, but has become something more than that because it is the officially recognised dialect, whose grammar we are all taught to write in. It is the English used in books teaching English as a foreign language.

The term Standard English does not relate to pronunciation. You can speak SE in any accent but SE is normally associated with a BBC or RP ('received pronunciation') accent. People refer to SE as *'Good English'*, *'The Queen's English'* and *'Proper English'*. But, as we saw in the History chapter, there is nothing inherently proper or good about it. It's just the dialect of English that has become the most prestigious and widely understood.

Although the vast majority of us *write* in SE, SE *speakers* are in a minority. It's difficult to say how much of a minority because there's no exact definition of Standard English. What is thought of as standard actually varies from area to area!

STANDARD ENGLISH SPEAKERS

SPEAKERS OF OTHER VARIETIES OF BRITISH ENGLISH

However, it is now

ALL A BIT MORE COMPLICATED THAN THAT because there isn't really one definitive Standard English. As soon as English began to travel across the globe, it began to change. There's now, for example, American SE and British SE; there's Australian SE, Canadian SE, Caribbean SE, East Asian SE and South Asian SE, and South African Standard English. Although these varieties have a great deal in common, they are nevertheless distinct.

NATIONAL VARIATION

Most national varieties are based on either a British English or American English model (or more likely on bits of both).

STANDARD AMERICAN ENGLISH (SAE) V STANDARD BRITISH ENGLISH (SBE)

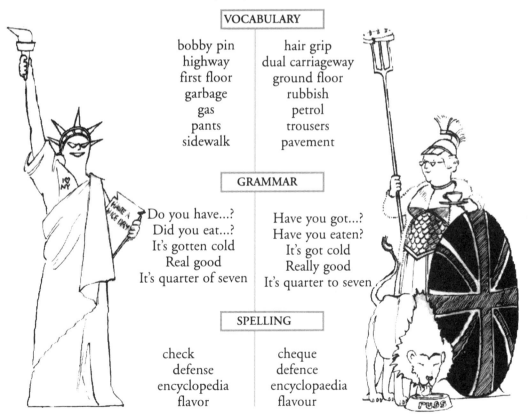

VOCABULARY	
bobby pin	hair grip
highway	dual carriageway
first floor	ground floor
garbage	rubbish
gas	petrol
pants	trousers
sidewalk	pavement

GRAMMAR	
Do you have...?	Have you got...?
Did you eat...?	Have you eaten?
It's gotten cold	It's got cold
Real good	Really good
It's quarter of seven	It's quarter to seven

SPELLING	
check	cheque
defense	defence
encyclopedia	encyclopaedia
flavor	flavour

Every English-speaking country has its own variety of English like these. As it's impossible for us to cover anywhere near all the different national varieties of English, we'll just take one other variety, Australian English, as an example, and examine its distinctive features and where they come from.

AUSTRALIAN ENGLISH

VOCABULARY:

1. CREATED IN AUSTRALIA:
There are many thousands of words in contemporary Australian English that did not arrive with the first British English speaking settlers. Lots of them describe the native flora and fauna (things that SBE had no words for) e.g., *bush* (natural vegetation), *bombora* (a navigable stretch of river with dangerous rocks in), *banksia, mallee, quandong, wattle* (types of tree). There are also lots of general words, e.g., *Gooday* (hello), *layby* (hire-purchase).

3. FROM AMERICAN ENGLISH:
As in many countries, American English is beginning to have a greater influence in Australia. Words like *stationwagon* (SBE *estate car*), *cookie* (SBE *biscuit*), *bank teller* (SBE *cashier*), *high school* (SBE *secondary school*), *truck* (SBE *lorry*) are now part of the language alongside SBE ones like *class* (SAE *grade*), *cinema* (SAE *movies*) and *petrol* (SAE *gas*).

2. FROM ABORIGINAL LANGUAGES:
There are some (not many) words that were borrowed from the aborigines, e.g., plant and animal names: *dingo, koala, kangaroo, wallaby, aburra* and place names: *Gnaraloo, Jimboomba, Widgiemooltha, Murwillumbah.*

GRAMMAR

Grammatically, Australian English is little different to SBE.

IRISH ENGLISH

However, there are quite a few features that show Irish influence, as about 30% of the population were of Irish origin by 1890 (Crystal 1995 p.352)

AUSTRALIAN ENGLISH	V	SBE
E.g. *youse*	=	*you (plural)*
He **mustn't** have seen her	=	he **can't** have seen her
But at the end of sentences (informal)	=	*I don't want it (though)*
*I don't want it **but***		

---

rEGIOnal vaRiatioN

Comparisons like those above tend to give the impression that **ALL** Americans say one thing and **ALL** British people say another. This is misleading, partly because different national varieties affect each other: American and British English have had increasing influence on each other over the last 25 years, especially American on British and partly because of regional variation: e.g., not all Americans would say *'it's quarter of seven'*:

Someone from East Pennsylvania would probably say,

'It's quarter of seven'.

But someone from Maine would probably say,

'It's quarter to seven'.

Whilst someone from South Carolina might say,

'It's quarter till seven'.

(Crystal 1995 p.313)

IT'S QUARTER TILL SEVEN

IT'S QUARTER OF SEVEN

IT'S QUARTER TO SEVEN

well here in California it's only 3.45

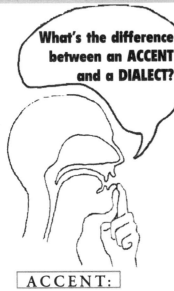

What's the difference between an ACCENT and a DIALECT?

ACCENT refers only to regional pronunciation. An English person with a northern accent will pronounce **bath** to rhyme with **sat** ('short a'), whereas an RP speaker rhymes it with **cart** ('long a').

DIALECT too concerns pronunciation, but it also covers vocabulary and grammar, so the different ways of saying 6:45p.m. in the previous page are dialectal differences.

ACCENT:

'The point of regional pronunciations is to enable one tribe of pronouncers to feel superior to another.' Philip Howard The Times 1993

Because the way we speak is closely tied up with our identity and our belonging to a certain social group, few people consider all accents to be equal. There is a social hierarchy, and so there is a language hierarchy. Since the 1960s, many experiments have been conducted into how people in England evaluate different accents. The results are very clear:

RP is by far and away the most prestigious accent. People not only prefer the accent but also make positive judgements about RP speakers' characters: they are considered more intelligent, determined, self-confident and ambitious. They are thought of as being wealthier and having better careers.

Next on the accent hierarchy come accents that are associated with nationality and education like Irish, Welsh and Scottish (educated Edinburgh accent).

Broad accents associated with the working class and large industrial cities seem to come the very bottom of the list. The four least liked accents are invariably Brummie (West Midlands/Birmingham), Cockney (London), Scouse (Liverpool) and Glaswegian (Glasgow).

ACCENTS AND DISCRIMINATION: Some surveys suggest that your accent actually affects things like your success in job interviews and your credibility as a defendant/witness in court (with accents from Liverpool, Glasgow and Birmingham being discriminated against).

Wot-ho!

Awright, Guv?

Oo arr.

LUCKILY, THERE ARE *SOME* POSITIVE POINTS TO HAVING A REGIONAL ACCENT. Research shows that those with regional accents are thought of as more good-natured, down to earth, talkative and humorous. And as we'll see in the class section, an RP accent is not ALWAYS the most prestigious; regional accents have a certain working class and male prestige.

Regional accents are heard far more today on the TV and radio than they were when the term BBC English was coined. Personalities like Ben Elton, Cilla Black, Lenny Henry, Billy Connolly, Victoria Wood and John Coles and programmes like East Enders, Coronation Street and Biker Grove have broadened the appeal of regional accents. But a hierarchy still exists. Can you imagine a broad cockney accent reading the news?

DIALECT:

Our traditional dialects are dying out. There are today very few people who speak in a broad dialect.

1. INCREASED MOBILITY
Children no longer grow up hearing only one dialect and then live all their lives in the same area. It is now normal, to move to a different part of the country to go to work.

2. COMPULSORY EDUCATION
This means that we all learn to read and write in Standard English.

3. THE MEDIA
Even if we were to stay in one village for our entire lives, we would still be exposed to standard English on the TV and radio and in the papers.

What most people now use is Standard English, with a sprinkling of regional words/grammatical forms rather than a broad dialect.
Some examples:

VOCABULARY:
If you went to school in Britain you probably know a dialect word for gym shoes, such as:

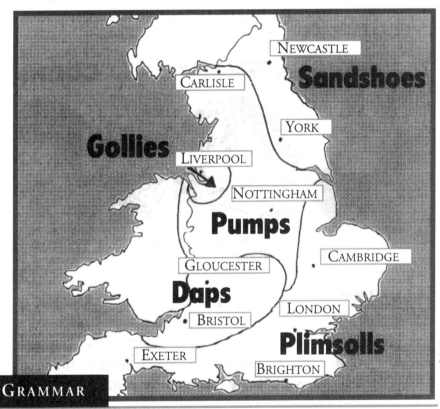

Map from Trudgill 199 p.102

STANDARD BRITISH ENGLISH	DIALECT
He likes her, he wants it	*He like her, he want it* (East Anglia)
I put, they cut	*I putten, they cutten* (Staffordshire)
I see him (on this single occasion)	*I sees him* (Somerset/Dorset)
I see him (on a regular basis)	*I do see him* (Somerset/Dorset)
I might be able to do it	*I might could do it* (Northumberland)
We'll wait until 5 p.m.	*We'll wait while 5 p.m.* (North Midlands)

VARIETY &
CHANGE   155

ESTUARY ENGLISH

While most regional dialects are gradually dying out, this one has recently begun to spread incredibly fast. The term 'Estuary English' was coined in the 80s to refer to the way in which English was being spoken in London and the surrounding South Eastern counties, especially Essex and Kent (the estuary in question being that of the river Thames).

WHAT IS IT?

It's a cross between RP and Cockney (the working class dialect spoken in the East End of London). If you draw a scale with highly conservative RP at one end and Cockney at the other, Estuary is smack in the middle.

RP   **ESTUARY**   **COCKNEY**

JOANNA LUMLEY   **BEN ELTON**   **FRANK BRUNO**

Estuary takes some of the characteristics of each and forms a compromise between the prestige that comes with RP and the down-to-earthness of Cockney. **Examples of Cockney usage found in Estuary English:**

PRONUNCIATION:	**GRAMMAR:**
Glottal Stop – replacing consonants at the end and in the middle of words (mainly 't's) with a stop in the throat, i.e.: *'Ga'wick airpor'* rather than 'Gatwick airport' **W instead of L** – i.e.: *'hiuw'* rather than *'hill'*	**Altered Negatives** – use of *'never'* to refer to a single occasion i.e.: *'You said I could borrow it'* *'I never did'* **Tag Questions** – used in a confrontational manner, i.e.: *'I said I was going, didn't I'* (not really a question when used this way) **Dropping 'ly'** – off the end of adverbs like 'slowly', i.e.: *'Don't turn too slow'*

But there are many bits of Cockney that don't make it into Estuary. These seem to be the most stigmatised, 'uneducated-sounding' features. For example, the use of double negatives (*'I ain't got no potatoes'*) is very consistent in Cockney, but much less so in Estuary. The same goes for the swapping of *th* with *f* and *v* in words like *this, that, thanks* and *thirty*, i.e. *vis, vat, fanks* and *firty*.

ORIGINS AND SPREAD

Estuary English developed gradually after World War Two, when a great number of Londoners moved away from the capital into the surrounding counties taking Cockney with them. In recent times, it has started to spread further afield. So far it has reached as far as Hull in the Northeast, Chester in the Northwest and Bristol in the Southwest, and it's still spreading.

WHY?

- BECAUSE OF COMMUTING – increasingly, businesspeople are travelling daily to and from London to work and taking the accents and vocabularies of their workplaces home with them.

... WE APOLOGISE ONCE AGAIN TO PASSENGERS FOR THE LATE RUNNING OF THIS SERVICE... THIS IS DUE TO LINGUISTIC RENOVATION WORK OVER THE WHOLE KENT & ESSEX AREA

London Charing Cross

- BECAUSE OF THE MEDIA – in recent years, there have been more and more TV and radio personalities with Estuary accents: Jonathan Ross, Janet Street Porter, Bob Hoskins, Michael Caine, Ben Elton and others who have given Estuary a good public image.

- BECAUSE OF SOCIAL CHANGE – lately there has also been a movement in the middle classes away from RP because it has actually been losing prestige. It is now more often seen as being pretentious rather than superior, and so people have steadily moved away from it in favour of the more down-to-earth Estuary.

There is some speculation about whether Estuary English will eventually replace RP as Britain's most influential accent.

Each generation alters its use of language in order to assert its difference and independence from its parent generation. Many young people's words are slang words that go in and out of fashion very quickly:

safe

sexy hot FUNKY

FIT **sorted** fab *neat*

cool groovy

SOUND

These are the sorts of words that soon sound very dated, especially when from the mouths of a parent or other adult. This is exactly their purpose: they separate those who know and use them from everyone else, and help to create a group identity.

EtHnic VaRiatioN

A good example of Ethnic variation within language is that of the existence of **Black English Vernacular (BEV)**. Spoken mainly in American inner-city ghettos, BEV was at first labelled as an illogical and incomplete form of expression born of cultural deprivation in the Black community. Since studies like that of William Labov in 1972, though, it has been recognized as an independent dialect of English – as expressive as any other.

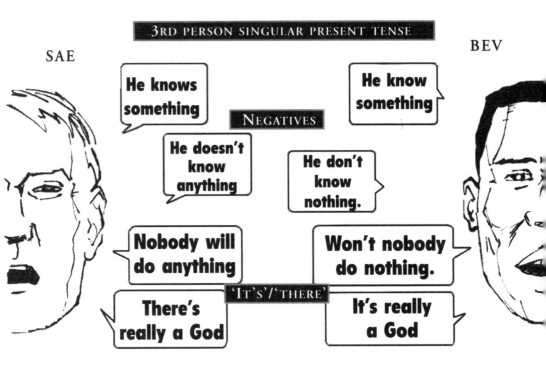

SAE

BEV

3RD PERSON SINGULAR PRESENT TENSE

He knows something

He know something

NEGATIVES

He doesn't know anything

He don't know nothing.

Nobody will do anything

Won't nobody do nothing.

'IT'S'/'THERE'

There's really a God

It's really a God

As you can see, BEV is not incomplete, it is simply different. In fact, in some ways it is more precise than SAE. Where a speaker of SAE might only say *'He's working'*, a speaker of BEV has the option of either *'He be working'*, meaning he is in work, generally speaking, or *'He working'*, meaning that he is merely working at the moment of the conversation.

Class Variation

The variety of language we use also signals our social class. There are certain variables which mean the same linguistically but say something different about us socially. The *postvocalic* r in New York City is a well-known example.

Labov in New York City

In New York, people will sometimes pronounce the r in words like *beard, car,* and *bear* and sometimes not. To begin with, linguists thought that this was purely random but Labov proved them wrong. William Labov studied who pronounced it, and when, where and how often they did so. This chart shows what he found:

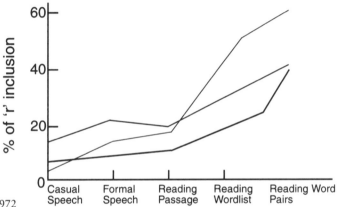

Based on Labov 1972

The bottom axis of the chart shows the different types of language Labov studied. They range from *casual speech*, the most spontaneous and informal, to *word pairs*, the most formal and thought out. The casual-speech rating is taken from a person's most natural speech, e.g., when they are talking about an emotive subject like an accident that happened to them, or digressing from a question (when they are so caught up in what they're saying, that they forget they're being recorded).

For their word-pair rating, they are asked to read two words that are distinguished only by the sound in question (so they more or less know what the linguist is looking at), e.g., *Source v sauce.*

WHAT DOES THE CHART SHOW?

Well, firstly it shows that pronouncing the *r* is the **prestigious variant** because in informal situations (CS, FS and RP) it is more common in upper-middle-class speech than in the lower classes', and because the more careful the speech style, the more each class used it (when people are self-conscious they pick the more prestigious way of speaking).

Secondly it shows language change in action. The lower-middle-class pronounces the *r* more frequently than the upper-middle-class in formal situations. This suggests that they are aware of its prestige and that due to a lack of confidence in their social standing they are trying too hard to talk like the upper MC. This is an example of what is called language change *'from above'*, meaning that the New Yorkers are aware that the pronounced *r* is prestigious and so are using it more and more. The opposite is a change *'from below'*, where the people using the new type of language are unaware that it's happening.

> The question is, if a variable like the post-vocalic r is prestigious, and people know it, why doesn't everybody use it all the time?

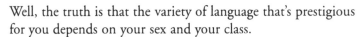

Well, the truth is that the variety of language that's prestigious for you depends on your sex and your class.

TRUDGILL IN NORWICH

Trudgill found that in Norwich pronouncing the ending '**ng**' on words like *walking* and *talking* is the prestigious variable. Like the *r* in New York, it is used more by each class than the one below and more in formal situations than informal ones.

So Trudgill's research seems at first glance to give exactly the same results as Labov's, but he took it a step further and looked at the sex as well as the class of the speaker.

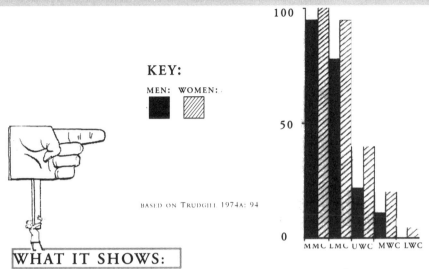

KEY:

MEN: WOMEN:

BASED ON TRUDGILL 1974A: 94

100

50

0

MMC LMC UWC MWC LWC

WHAT IT SHOWS:

1. Women of each class use the prestige variant more than men of the same class.

2. Using the nonstandard variable is not only a working-class thing, it's also a male thing.

Many other studies have found this same pattern.

NEXT, Trudgill did what are called self-evaluation tests. That is, he presented the people in his survey with a prestigious and stigmatised pronunciation and asked them to say which they thought they normally used. He already knew the truth from his survey, of course, so he was able to compare how people actually spoke with how they thought they did. What they were actually telling him was how they'd like to talk.

He found that **women of all classes tend to over-report** (i.e., claim that they are using the prestigious variant when actually they don't) whilst the **men of all classes tend to under-report** (i.e., claim they used the non-standard form when in fact they use the prestigious one). This suggests that men and women (as well as the upper and lower classes) were aiming to speak a different type of language.

OVERT AND COVERT PRESTIGE

Standard English and prestigious forms (e.g., *postvocalic r, ng* in Norwich)

Regional varieties, non-standard forms

Overt prestige is the prestige that comes with using the type of language that is nationally recognised and used in official and educational contexts. Speakers who use standard English are therefore considered well educated, intelligent and so on, because they are using the *correct* and *best* version of English. It is easy to see why the middle classes use this variety of language.

Covert prestige, on the other hand, comes from *not* identifying with the institutionalised standard (e.g., the young people's language described above has anti-establishment covert prestige). It is the prestige that comes with group loyalty and solidarity. Working-class speakers signal solidarity with their class and region by sticking to vernacular (non-standard) norms.

> So why the male/female difference?

One theory is that women, like the LMC, are socially insecure and so are more careful to use the overtly socially prestigious forms than men.

Another is that working-class, vernacular language is associated with being rough and tough. In one survey people were asked to rate how well they thought recorded speakers would do in a street fight. Those with strong regional accents came out on top every time. These traits are considered macho and so men veer towards talking like this and women veer away from it. Some linguists have also commented that standard forms are associated with (normally) female schoolteachers and suggested that boys reject this female model more than girls do.

It is however worth considering that everybody uses vernacular forms more in informal situations. We're all more likely to use accent and dialect when at home amongst friends and Standard English when in a more formal situations like a job interview or a courtroom. It would be misleading to consider vernacular forms male and SE as female.

Because the language we use signals our membership of different social groups, it can easily be used – consciously and unconsciously – to include or exclude people from a group.

ACCOMMODATION:

This is what sometimes happens when we are talking to someone we like/agree with who has a different accent: we gradually alter our accent so that it becomes more like theirs. We are signalling affinity.

The opposite occurs if we meet someone we dislike or disagree with: we exaggerate the differences in our speech to show that we have nothing in common and are not part of the same group.

LABOV IN MARTHA'S VINEYARD:

Labov's research on this small island three miles off mainland America is a clear example of how we subconsciously change our language to identify ourselves with one group and not with another. It is an example of language changing subconsciously from below.

The Situation: The island had a
permanent population of about 6000 people. Every summer, much to these locals' disgust, another 40,000 'summer people' flocked to the island.

Labov discovered that there was a sound change in progress in the speech of the rural, permanent population: the vowel sound [au] in words like *out, trout* and *house* was moving towards a [əu] sound, and the [ai] sound in words like *white, like* and *night* was moving towards a [ə i] sound.

As in the New York City research, Labov interviewed people and recorded their pronunciation in different speech styles. This time he found that the islanders were not aware of their speech changing: in more formal styles, they did not use the prestigious pronunciation any more often.

He also discovered the following:
1. The people who used the new vowels most were the island's old fishermen.
2. After them, the change was affecting islanders in their 30s and 40s most.

SO WHAT WAS GOING ON?

It turned out that the vowel sounds weren't new at all, they had for a long time been present in the speech of the fishermen. They were in fact part of a conservative old-fashioned way of speaking. Labov suggests that the islanders were reverting to this old pronunciation because they were subconsciously signaling an affinity with the island's traditional values. A non-standard pronunciation was gaining covert prestige.

The fishermen were the group who were most opposed to the summer visitors. They subconsciously exaggerated their non-standard pronunciation to establish themselves as a group and to distance themselves from the outsiders. The other islanders (especially those in their 30s/40s) saw these fishermen as true islanders. They subconsciously wanted to show that they admired these men and what they stood for, and that they were part of the same group of true islanders. So, they gradually began to imitate the way the fishermen spoke. (Research: Labov 1972)

JARGON: Every occupation, hobby, sport, etc. has its own jargon (technical language). Jargon is a variety of language that is well known for excluding/including people. In fact, the word **jargon** now has another, negative meaning: it is very often used to mean **obscure, pretentious, unnecessarily technical language used to baffle and exclude** the uninitiated. Here are some examples of jargon in use.

First, and most important, although DOS was arguably a suitable OS for the early 8088, It clearly became inadequate for the 80286 (or above) systems as it made no use of the improved hardware on offer. DOS supports a single user running a single program in real mode using only 640Kb of memory, regardless of how much memory the machine has. It uses no virtual memory, no multiprogramming and no swapping – all perfectly reasonable facilities to have in an 80286-based machine.
(*Personal Computer World*, May 1997, p.103)

Allington confers the power of this bureaucratic, neutralised voice upon his constructions of artifactual decoys in order to slyly enter the province of the cultural institution. This 'voice' becomes a camouflage for the work as it enters into the archival framework of representation and pictorialisation. In this sense, the object becomes the symbolic icon of the dialectic of positive and negative hermeneutics as expressed through the interplay of various ideological 'contents'.
(*Art and Design Profile 9*, 1988, p.12)

Whereas the jargon in the first extract is necessary to discuss the specialist field of computing, that in the second serves only to exclude the average reader from whatever it is the writer is on about (it serves no practical purpose).

PART TWO

LanGuage Change

Is the appalling speech that buzzes about our ears today part of the general malaise? *

...been shocked by the bad grammar and pronunciation of many newsreaders and other present-ers on BBC radio and tele-vision. A mistake that par-ticularly irritates me is the lack of understanding of what is the subject of a sentence and that the subject of a sentence should agree with the verb. The fol-lowing is a recent example from a BBC1 newsreader: 'War and famine *has* resulted in many deaths.' 'War and famine' constitute a plural subject. The sentence should begin 'War and famine *have* resulted.'

I have other pet hates. One is the almost universal substitu-tion of 'bought' (the past tense of 'buy') for 'brought' (the past tense of 'bring'). Maybe I am just getting old, but BBC English is certainly no longer a model to... followed.

...speaking, now prevalent among young television presenters, *

...hobbyhorse is the use of 'dif-ferent to' when the user means 'different from'. I have never been able to understand how this has been given credibility. I have also noticed recently that BBC reporters are frequently misusing the word 'if' when they mean 'whether'.

If your venture does some-thing to highlight these failings, it will be worth while. *

To mention only one exam-ple, we hear at least two split infinitives a day. I wrote to the BBC on this matter a year ago, only to be informed by some minion working for the cor-poration that the English lan-guage is changing. I am not aware of this and neither are any other educated people in this country. The only change is the increasingly slovenly use of speech. *

AN EDUCATION professor who says the present generation of schoolchildren has grown up un-able to tell 'laying down' from 'lying down', and regularly per-petrates illiteracies, is calling for the foundation of a National Lan-guage Authority to regulate Eng-lish language use.

The Authority – made up of scholars, novelists, the editor of the *Oxford English Dictionary* and professional writers – would is-sue directives on the use of 'whom', 'whose' and phrases such as 'he ran quicker'. *

...transmissions are largely pre-sented by young people who have an insolent command of appalling English. *

(* Sunday Times 1993)
(* Independent on Sunday 17th Aug 1997)

Word perfect

From Mr G. D. Ashley

Sir, Today, at different times whilst listening to the radio, I have heard the descriptions 'computer literate' and 'computer illiterate' on at least six occasions. It would seem to a person of lowly scientific training that the words 'computerate' and 'incomputerate' would fulfil these functions more succinctly.

Yours faithfully
(alas incomputerately),
G. D. ASHLEY,

Word perfect

From Mr Kevin Grant

Sir, I was glad to read that Mr G. D. Ashley (letter, July 25) has found his way to the terms 'computerate' and 'incomputerate'. They should indeed be validated by inclusion in the lexicon.

He might like to add my term for describing most of us: 'nincomputerate', substantively a 'nincompute'

Yours sincerely,
KEVIN GRANT

Word perfect

From Mr Ted Whybrew

Sir, Mr Kevin Grant's new term 'nincompute' (letter, July 30) is to be welcomed, but he seems to use it to describe someone with an extreme form of 'incomputeracy'.

Does it not better describe those individuals whose working and social lives are wholly dominated by webs, modems and their like?

Yours faithfully,
TED WHYBREW

From Mr John Gudgeon

Sir, As the French call the computer l'ordinateur, why not 'ordinate' or 'inordinate' for those who understand them or don't?

Yours sincerely,
JOHN GUDGEON

Word perfect

From Mr Colin Lester

Sir, 'Ordinate' is surely the right substitute for 'computer-literate' (letter, August 2), since so many of us are subordinate to these machines — except for hackers, of course, who are insubordinate.

Yours faithfully,
C. J. LESTER

(Times letter Column 1997)

Language *matters*...

It sparks discussion and debate at all levels of society. People everywhere care about how it is used and often have strong opinions about what good/bad language is. Prescriptivism didn't die with the 18th century grammarians, there's a bit of it in all of us. We'd all like to control language in some way. Even people who claim to be descriptive and open minded have their pet hates. Can you honestly say that there is no example of language use that makes you cringe: whether it's your son saying *'bu'er'* instead of *butter*, people using *'less'* in place of *'fewer'* or the greengrocers' apostrophe?

And is it?

What people's complaints often come down to is language change. Adults moan that their children don't speak as they did, just as *their* parents did before them. Many people claim that standards are declining and that change is a bad thing, a result of laziness or sloppiness. It's evidence that language is decaying.

NO. Language change will always occur whilst a language is alive and in use. Social and geographical variations play a large part in language change: as soon as a variation on Standard English exists, there is the possibility that it will spread and replace the old form. Social pressures like the need to identify with your age, class and region as well as the desire to move up a class or change your image, help new terms to spread, as does people's increased mobility – commuting to work, or visiting family who've moved to a different part of the country.

So, because language change is so closely linked to social change, trying to stop language change is futile. Throughout history people have tried and failed. The Académie Française, for example, is trying very hard to prevent English words entering the French language. Despite their efforts though, most French people say things like *le parking, le weekend, le hotdog, le walkman* and *le pub*.

So how does language change?

We'll look at how language changes in three parts: **lexical change** (words), **grammatical change** and **sound change**. In each section, we'll cover a small selection of common complaints about change.

LeXical Change

Lexical change is probably the aspect of language change that we are most aware of. We all know that over the past few years the word *gay* has gained an extra meaning *(homosexual)* which will soon completely wipe out the old one *(cheerful)*. And we are all conscious of new words that have recently entered the language, e.g., *'alcopop'*, *'CD ROM'*, *'rollover week'*.

NEOLOGISMS (NEW WORDS)

Here are some of the ways in which neologisms are made:

1. BORROWING: a word from a foreign language becomes part of the English Language, e.g. *Karaoke* (from Japanese), *pyjamas* (from Hindi).

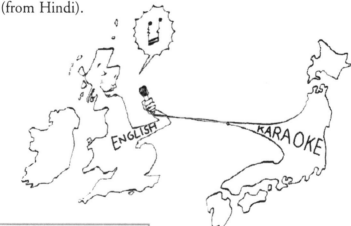

2. COMPOUNDING: two or more existing words are stuck together, e.g., *takeover, bittersweet, girlfriend, couchpotato, crybaby, mother-of-pearl.*

3. BLENDING: two or more existing words are merged, e.g., *ginormous* (*giant + enormous*), *brunch* (*breakfast + lunch*), *breathalyser* (*breath + analyser*), *smog* (*smoke + fog*), *motel* (*motor + hotel*).

4. DERIVATION: a word (an acronym) is formed from the initial letters of other words, e.g., *dinky* (dual income no kids), *nimby* (not in my back yard), *laser* (light amplification by simulated emission of radiation), *scuba* (self-contained underwater breathing apparatus).

5. ABBREVIATION: a word is shortened, e.g., *fax* (*facsimile*), *bike* (*bicycle*), *flu* (*influenza*), *celeb* (*celebrity*), *gym* (*gymnasium*), *bus* (*autobus*), *memo* (*memorandum*), *maths* (*mathematics*).

6. ROOT CREATING:
Words are made up entirely (often for phonological effect), e.g., *blurb* (coined in 1907 by Gelett Burgess, the American Humorist) *nerd, dork*.

7. CONVERSION: a word transfers from one word class to another, e.g., verb → noun: *to refill* → *a refill*, noun → verb: *a hammer* → *to hammer*, adjective → verb: *dirty* → *to dirty*.

8. BACKFORMATION: new words are made by removing affixes from old ones, e.g., *editor* was adapted to *to edit*, and *surrealist* led to *surreal*. Sometimes it is a false assumption that brings about new words, e.g., *beefburger* and later *chicken burger* and **vegeburger** were backformed from **hamburger**, which was not a '*burger*' made of ham, but a dish named after Hamburg.

I PREFER TO BE MUNCHEN ON A FRANKFURTER

9.EPOYNM: A new word is created from a person's name (often the person who popularised or invented it) e.g. the *Plimsoll line* from Samuel Plimsoll, the *leotard* from the acrobat Jules Leotard.

Many new words are coined every day but the vast majority of them are **NONCES** (temporary words that never properly enter the language). They are often created to solve an immediate communication problem or to play on current affairs. It is extremely difficult to predict which new words will be seized upon (perhaps by the papers) and soon enter the dictionaries, and which will never be heard of again.

Take for example, the epoynm coined in the early 90s: **to bobbitt.**
In June 1992 Lorena Bobbitt cut off her husband John Wayne Bobbitt's penis. The papers came up with the verb *to bobbitt* (meaning something like *'to vengefully remove one's husbands penis'*) At the time no one could have known whether this new word was to be a nonce that would disappear as fast as it had been coined or whether it would stay with us and enter the dictionaries.

As it turns out, the word is still alive. It is used literally and figuratively (meaning something like *'to emasculate / remove status from'*) and looks like a strong candidate for dictionary inclusion.

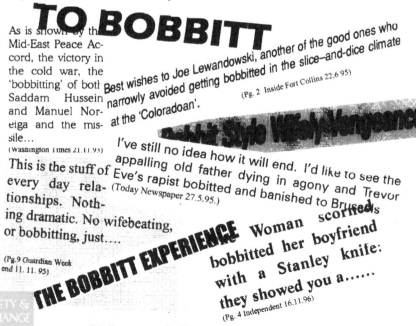

TO BOBBITT

As is shown by the Mid-East Peace Accord, the victory in the cold war, the 'bobbitting' of both Saddam Hussein and Manuel Noreiga and the missile...
(Washington Times 21.11.95)

This is the stuff of every day relationships. Nothing dramatic. No wifebeating, or bobbitting, just....

(Pg.9 Guardian Week end 11.11.95)

Best wishes to Joe Lewandowski, another of the good ones who narrowly avoided getting bobbitted in the slice–and-dice climate at the 'Coloradoan'.
(Pg. 2 Inside Fort Collins 22.6 95)

I've still no idea how it will end. I'd like to see the appalling old father dying in agony and Trevor Eve's rapist bobbitted and banished to Brussels
(Today Newspaper 27.5.95.)

THE BOBBITT EXPERIENCE Woman scorned bobbitted her boyfriend with a Stanley knife: they showed you a......
(Pg. 4 Independent 16.11.96)

CHANGES TO OLD WORDS

Here are some of the ways in which words' meanings change:

Meaning Extension: <u>a word's meaning widens</u>; e.g., *bird* used to mean only *'young bird'*. In Latin, *'virtue'* could only be applied to men. In medieval times, the word *'hierarchy'* was used only to rank different sorts of angels, in the 17th century it was extended to the ranking of clergymen and today it is used to rank anything.

Meaning Narrowing: <u>a word's usage becomes more specialised</u>, e.g., *meat* (Old English *mete*) used to mean all food, *deer* once described any animal, *girl* meant young person (of either sex) and *to starve* (Old English *steorfan*) used to mean to die by any means.

Amelioration: <u>a word gains positive connotations</u>, e.g., *sophisticated* used to mean not *highly developed/cultured/worldly-wise* but *artificial*. *Mischievous* used to mean *disastrous* but now has a much less grave meaning: *'playfully annoying'*.

Pejoration: <u>a word develops negative connotations</u>, e.g., words about women (discussed in previous chapter) such as *mistress*, *madam*, and *dame*. Or *notorious*, which used to mean *famous*, whereas today it means *infamous*.

AND NOW FOR THE COMPLAINTS...

Did you know that contemporary English uses words borrowed from over 120 languages? (Crystal 1995 p.126) Many of these borrowings date as far back as Anglo-Saxon times. Words we would never think of as foreign were borrowed sometime in the past (see page 30). This is one of the reasons that English is such an expressive language with so many synonyms:

ask (Old English)	**question** (French)	**interrogate** (Latin)

Americanisms particularly annoy many British people. Some seem to see British English as the purer, more 'correct' and more historically sound variety. The truth is that SAE and SBE have just retained different elements of their linguistic past. For instance, *Gotten* and *I guess* were once widely used in Britain, too. Shakespeare often used '**I guess**' for I think, and in the 17th century, *gotten* was used in England as it is now in America. It is actually the British English versions that are new.

Also, those people who complain about new, more obvious Americanisms are probably unaware of how many they themselves use. Many common, useful phrases like *'To cave in'*, *'to take a back seat'*, *'to belittle'*, *'governmental'*, *'lengthy'* and *'law abiding'* originated in the U.S. (Burchfield 1985 p.163)

NEW MEANINGS FOR OLD WORDS E.G., GAY, SAD, CHEERS

NEW-FANGLED WORDS E.G., THOSE THAT COME FROM COMPUTING – TO ACCESS, TO INPUT

The thing is, there never was a golden age of language when all word meanings were correct. It's not inherently correct for gay to mean cheerful. The connotations or meanings of words are constantly shifting.

In 1200 *nice* meant **stupid**
In 1500 *nice* meant **accurate**
Silly once meant **blessed**
Vulgar once meant **ordinary**

Language has to change to be useful to us. If we all stuck rigidly to the vocabulary Shakespeare used and never created any new words how could we hope to discuss modern life? A sample of the new words created each decade shows how developments in modern living give rise to new words.

1940s:
radar, nylon stockings, squat, bikini

1950s:
Do-it-yourself, H-bomb, nuke, cosmonaut, senior citizen

1960s:
acid, baby boom, bar code, biodegradable, brain-drain, gay, generation gap, groupie, jogging, teenybopper, theme park, unisex

1970s:
BMX, chairperson, chat-show, floppy disk, head-banger, punk, Page Three girl, slam-dunk

1980s:
aerobics, breakdance, CD, date rape, Filofax, karaoke, rave, Walkman, yuppie

GRAMMATICAL CHANGE

Grammatical change tends to be slower than lexical change. Perhaps the most noticeable thing that happens is a process of change by analogy, or

NEATENING

This refers to the fact that, over time, irregularities in the language gradually get ironed out.

E.g., plurals:

In Old English, there were many ways of forming a plural:

cwene = queens	*scipu* = ships	*hundas* = dogs
suna = suns	*eagan* = eyes	*word* = words

Then over many centuries, they gradually decreased, until by Shakespeare's day there were two main ways: *adding an 's'*, and *adding an 'n'*, e.g., *eyen* (eyes) and *housen* (houses). Today the plural ending is nearly always an *s* (some exceptions remain: *sheep, men, oxen*). The language has gradually neatened up because irregular words were treated like regular ones until they too became regular.

Verbs

A similar thing has happened to English verbs. In Old English, there were three types of verb:

Strong: those that make a past tense by changing a vowel: *I ride, I rode*.

Weak: those that make a past tense by adding *-ed*: *I love, I loved*.

Irregular: those whose form can't be predicted by rules: *I go, I went*.

We still have these three types of verb, but the weak kind are now much more common than they were in Old English. They are our regular verbs, and we have thousands of them with only about 300 irregular ones left. This is because over time, the structures of many irregular/strong verbs were altered by analogy to make them the same as regular ones. For example, the strong verb *to reap* (past tense *rope*) gradually became the weak verb it is today (past tense *reaped*).

A similar thing happened to lots of other verbs, including *help, bow, climb, walk, burn* and *step*. New verbs, such as those borrowed from other languages, were also logically fitted into the pattern of regular verbs, e.g., *elect, fuse, suggest* and *insert*.

You can still see the force of analogy today when people, especially children, say *'I knowed', 'I shooted', 'I runned'*, and so on.

One of the reasons that grammatical change is slower than lexical change is that people have a greater resistance to grammatical change. Words can come and go but to change the grammar of a language is to touch its core, its structure. For this reason, the most popular subject of letters to newspapers bemoaning declining standards is grammar.

SOME UNPOPULAR CONSTRUCTIONS:

ENDING A SENTENCE WIH A PREPOSITION, E.G., 'WHICH BOX DID HE PUT IT IN?' (SHOULD BE 'IN WHICH BOX DID HE PUT IT?')

DOUBLE NEGATIVES E.G., 'I DIDN'T HAVE NONE'

SPLIT INFINITIVES, E.G., 'IT TAKES A LONG TIME TO FULLY MASTER THEM ALL' (should be 'FULLY TO MASTER...')

USE OF 'DIFFERENT TO' RATHER THAN 'DIFFERENT FROM'

INCORRECT PERSONAL PRONOUNS, E.G., SAYING 'IT IS ME' RATHER THAN 'IT IS I'

Believe it or not, all of these complaints go back to the idiosyncratic rules made up by 18th-century rulebook writers like Robert Lowth (see the History chapter). Many of them are a pointless attempt to make English fit into the rules of the much admired language, Latin. For example, it was decreed that we should say *it is I* because in Latin the verb *to be* is followed by the nominative case, but this is totally irrelevant to English which has a much reduced case system. English writers from Chaucer to Shakespeare to modern day have been splitting infinitives and ending sentences with prepositions and the language hasn't fallen apart. What right have we (or Robert Lowth) to say this is wrong?

That may be, but you can't pretend that all the grammatical rules that are being broken today are irrelevant prescriptive ones. What about:

Plural words being used in the singular e.g. 'The media is...' 'Graffiti is...'

EXHIBIT A

If you think about it those aren't really examples of rule-breaking, they're rule following, an extension of the plural neatening described above: Now that the rule for plurals is *'add an s'*, it is logical to assume that words like *'media'* which don't end in an s are singular. Eventually they may become totally regular and fit into the system: *'the medias are'*...

It's natural for us to feel that this is incorrect but who knows, perhaps in 100 years the old form (singular *medium* ➔ plural *media*) will have been forgotten and everyone will be using the 'incorrect' one. Just as today we are all unwittingly using *chickens* as the plural of *chicken* – until the 16th/17th century, the correct form was *chickenu.*

Neatening has also affected many other words like *pease* (as in *'pease pudding hot'*), which was a singular word, but because it sounded like a plural, it came to be treated as one and a new word for the singular was created: *pea.* The word *dice* is another example; it was the plural of a *die* but is now often used as the singular with the new (logical and regular) plural *'dices'.* Other words like *index* (*indexes* not *indices*), *formula* (*formulas* not *formulae*), and *cactus* (*cactuses* not *cacti*) are following the same pattern.

WHEN THE CHICKENS START A PERCHING ON THE CACTUSES, IT'S A SURE SIGN THAT IT'LL START RAINING PEAS.

no more moonshine for me

SOUND CHANGE

Some sound changes also follow the principle of neatening. Different languages make use of different sounds, but the selection of sounds a language uses is not a random one. Languages tend to be quite symmetrical, so that sounds often appear in pairs. If a sound is not paired up, then it's a likely candidate for neatening.

FRICATIVES:

Fricatives are sounds made by partially interrupting the passage of air from the mouth: *sh, th, s, f, v, z,* etc. They can be divided up into *voiced* (sounds in which the vocal cords are vibrated) and *unvoiced* (sounds in which they're not). In the 18th century there were eight fricatives in English:

VOICELESS	{f} fish	{θ} thin	{s} song	{ʃ} ship	{h} hen
VOICED	{v} van	{ð} then	{z} zebra		

based on Jean Aitchison 1991 p.140

As you can see, two of them, *sh* and *h,* didn't have partners. Since the 19th century, sound changes have been occurring to neaten these two loners up.

First, a partner was created for *sh* [ʃ] The new sound *szh* [ʒ] came from borrowing French words like *beige* and *genre* and from a new pronunciation of English words like *pleasure, measure, leisure,* and *treasure,* which were once pronounced as if they ended in *-zer.*

And now *h,* instead of gaining a partner, is showing signs of disappearing. It is already virtually non-existent in dialects like Cockney and Estuary. So, what with the spread of Estuary English, it may not be long before no *h's* are pronounced anywhere and the language has a neatly balanced set of fricatives!

HOW SOUND CHANGES SPREAD:

A sound change does not sweep the country overnight, affecting all words at once. It spreads gradually by a process known as LEXICAL DIFFUSION: the new pronunciation starts small in a few common words. A limited number of people use it sporadically alongside the old pronunciation (in Labov's post-vocalic r research, a speaker would pronounce the *r* in a word one day but not the next). Gradually, the new pronunciation ousts the old as more and more people consistently pronounce those few common words in the new way. Once established in those words, the new sound filters through the language word by word and person by person until most words have taken up the change. Most people barely notice that anything has changed.

A CHANGE IN PROGRESS:
Take a look at the following words that end in a vowel followed by *ry*:

century, burglary, bravery, adultery, cursory, prudery, robbery, slavery, exemplary, scenery, gallery, summary

All of these words are pronounced almost as if they rhymed with *furry* – with a short nondescript sound (a '**schwa**') in place of the last vowel. In some words of the same type, however, a sound change is happening: the schwa is being dropped. Words like, *every, nursery, factory* and *battery,* are often pronounced as if there were no last vowel at all: *evry, nursry, factry* and *battry*. This sound change has become established in these everyday words. In slightly less common words like *delivery, history, mystery* and *primary*, it occurs sporadically and the least common words like those above have not yet been affected.

(based on Jean Aitchison 1991 pg. 78 and 140

Abbreviation e.g., dropping 'H's at the beginning of words as in 'our 'ouse'

The Glottal stop e.g., saying bu'er instead of butter

Dropping *'h's* is something we notice because it is an indicator of class, but it's actually surprising how many other sounds get dropped from rapid speech. We just don't realise we're doing it: who says *handbag* and not *hambag*, or *got to go* and not *gotta go*? Dropping sounds is a perfectly normal result of fast, fluent speech and not a sign of sloppiness.

However, as we discussed above, *'h's* are slightly different, because they are slowly being dropped from **all** speech, not just fast speech. They may disappear altogether one day, who knows? If they do, they won't be the first sound to go: in the fifteenth century, for example, the *k* in words like *knight* and *knit* was pronounced.

This pronunciation is widely thought of as easier than pronouncing 'a proper t' and so it's condemned as lazy/sloppy. This is a fallacy. It actually takes a great deal of muscular tension to say 'Be'y 'ad a bi' of bi'er bu'er' (Betty had a bit of bitter butter) (Jean Aitchison 1996 Reith lectures).

So, when you see the wider picture of how language changes, how it has changed in the past and will continue changing for as long as it is used, it is very clear that change is not a sign of decline or decay. Change is not a new phenomenon that is attacking a once pure language. All of the changes underway today have parallels in history. There is no evidence to suggest that language is decaying and standards declining. In fact, change often works to neaten the language.

Change is natural and inevitable.

The most important thing about change is that it makes language flexible enough to cope with changes in society.

Language's flexibility and capacity to adapt is illustrated by a look at

🞷 The effect of computers, the internet and other new communications technology on English

Trash

1. THE SPREAD OF AMERICAN ENGLISH

In the second half of the 20th century, America has dominated software and hardware production. This means that to get the cutting edge on computer technology or programs, you have to buy the ones that use American English. Versions in other languages often come later, and are slower or more prone to error.

English is also by far the most used language on the Internet. This is partly because American users are in a majority in many areas of the Internet and partly because it is normally the language used across borders, as a shared second language between different nations.

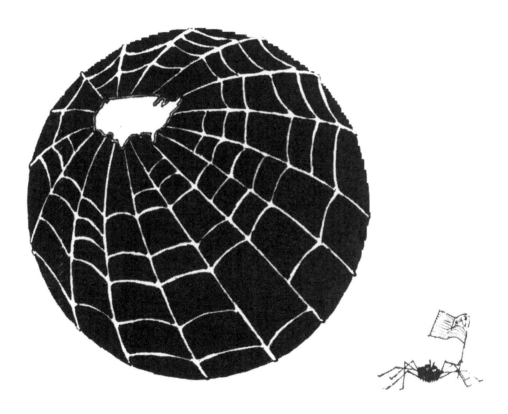

US VOCABULARY: many computer-related terms come to other varieties of English (and other languages) from American English because that is where most of the technology comes from. In England we have *TV programmes* but computer progr*ams*. We have slipped *discs* but *computer disks*, etc.

2. NEW VOCABULARY

Computers have led to the creation of vast amounts of new vocabulary. **Some words are created to describe the new technology and all that comes with it:**

Floppy disk = a small diskette for storing magnetically coded computer information (software).

Hard drive = a computer's internal software storage facility – another kind of larger magnetic disk housed within the body of the computer.

CD-ROM = Compact Disc Read Only Memory (a CD for use on computers).

Email = electronic mail. Messages sent via the internet to specific computer addresses.

Glass = fibre optic cable used to heighten the efficiency of internet connections.

And some words arise to accommodate the new ways language is being used on-line (much of which comes in the form of acronyms for ease of typing), e.g.:

MARTIAN MAIL = an email that arrives so long after it was sent that it seems to have come via Mars.

CYBRARIAN = a digital librarian, an on-line information researcher.

LURKER = someone who reads chat-line conversations but does not participate.

MEATSPACE = the real world where people actually live and things like eating and sleeping go on.

PONA = Person of No Account. Someone who is not on-line.

PEBCAK = Problem Exists Between Chair and Keyboard. Used by telephone technical support workers to mean that it is the user rather than the computer system that is at fault.

JOOTT = Just One Of Those Things. Acronym used to describe problems that appear in a system and then disappear without any explanation.

1. PARTICIPATIVE READING: electronic texts make the reader more active: they are not reading fixed, static texts, but texts they themselves can manipulate on screen. **Hypertexts**, for example, are documents where one piece of writing has a link with others (e.g., CD-ROM encyclopaedias), so that it is the reader who chooses their own path through the text depending on what they click on with their mouse.

2. SPEECH/WRITING? New communications technology (since as far back as the telephone) has been breaking down the traditional boundaries between Speech and writing:

–Speech was once ephemeral and writing concrete. Now answering machines, dictaphones, tape recorders and video cameras have made it possible to record and transmit speech over long distances.

–Speech was once the only immediate, interactive form of communication, whilst written communication was considered, and answered, at a later date. When people 'chat' on the Internet, or send e-messages to each other, they are both at their computers and they have a conversation in real time, where questions and responses follow immediately. It is more like a phone conversation than a letter, but it is still written language.

–Speech is normally informal and spontaneous and so less grammatically correct, full of incomplete sentences, mispronunciations, etc., whilst writing is formal, planned and grammatically accurate. On chat lines, however, people write in the informal vocabulary and grammar of spoken language. For the sake of speed they rarely correct spelling or grammatical errors.

4. NEW RELATIONSHIPS/IDENTITIES

ANONYMITY: One of the most interesting things about conversations on the Internet is that the people talking to each other lose almost all of the features of language that define their social class, ethnic origins, age, and so on. Most people who log on do not use their own name; they are not speaking so they have no accent to define them regionally or socially. The person who you're talking to could be next door or a continent away. How this affects interactions is as yet unclear. Many people find it much easier to participate in an electronic discussion than in a face-to-face one. It equalises people so that shy people don't get shouted down, or miss a chance to say something.

(based on Ch.3 of Goodman and Goddard 1996 by Simon Yates)

ENGLISH IN THE FUTURE

The future of the English language is a very emotive subject. For centuries people have been predicting both the ruin and the glorious future of English (going as far as total disappearance at one end and world domination at the other).

Some people predict that the many varieties of English will move farther and farther apart until their speakers can no longer understand each other. The different varieties will become new languages and English will be dead.

Others say that the different varieties will gradually move closer together, resulting in a single Global Standard English that is spoken by all.

GLOBAL STANDARD ENGLISH

OPPOSING FORCES:

English is being pulled in these two opposite directions:

TOGETHER: things like international travel, international press coverage and satellite broadcasting, multinational business enterprise and intergovernmental cooperation are all contributing to the spread and recognition of a Standard English.

APART: the geographical and cultural differences between all the places English is spoken leads to diversity. English picks up useful bits of neighbouring languages. Speakers create new words to describe local life, practices and cultural issues, as well as things like indigenous plants and animals. These new or borrowed words/grammatical structures are irrelevant to English speakers elsewhere so diversity is maintained. The pressure to forge a national or group identity strengthens this tendency too.

It seems more than likely that these opposing forces will lead to some sort of compromise. Perhaps local variations will exist at the same time as an international standard, each being used in different situations.

Erm, well...
that's the end.

A

Accomodation 166-167
Académie Française 36
accents 152-4
affective tags 94, 98
Age Variation 159
alliteration 138
alveolar sounds 60
American English 186-8
American linguistics 39
Americanisms 176
androcentricism 106-14
Angles, The 15
Anglo-Normans 22-6
Anglo-Saxons 15, 18-19, 24
animal communications 3-4
approval adjectives 89
Atkinson, Max 137
Australian English 150-1
Australopithecus Africanus 5-6

B

Bailey 33
Baldwin, James 117
Barr and Atkins 99-100
Black English Vernacular (BEV) 160
Bloomfield, Leonard 39
Bolinger, Dwight 123
brain control of speech 4
Brend, Ruth 93
Brown and Levison 97
Berko and Brown 59
Brown Cazden and Belligi 71

C

Cameron and Coates 102, 101
caretaker languages 75-9
caretaker reinforcement 70-1
Carmicheal, Hogan and Walter 132
cases (word endings) 19-20
Cawdrey, Robert 33
Caxton, William 29
Celtic language 15, 18
Chaucer, Geoffrey 26, 27
children's language
        acquisition devices 80-4
        acquisition theories 66-74
        caretaker language 75-9
        developmental stages 43-65
        grammar 50, 51-5
        negatives 55

phonology 44, 45, 50, 59-63
pragmatics 44, 45, 50, 64-5
psycholinguistic model 82-4
questions 54
semantics 50, 56-8
Chomsky, Noam 40, 80-1, 135
Christianity 18, 19
'claptraps' 137
Clark, Hutcheson and van Buren 57
Coates, J. 101, 104
cockney dialect 156-7
commercial language 139
common cognates 12, 13
communications and language
development 30, 189-90
competitive conversations 101-5
consonant clusters 62
conversations
        with children 64-5
        co-operative versus competitive 101-5
        mixed sex 103-4
        Internet 190
        sexual differences in 91-105
        co-operative conversations 101-5
correct standard pronunciation 93
correction resistance 71
covert prestige 164-5
critical periods, in language
acquisition 70
Cro-Magnons 7-8, 10
Cruttenden, Alan 62-3
Crystal, David 61, 71, 64

D

Darwin, Charles 10
Defoe, Daniel 36
descriptive grammars 39
descriptive linguistics 38-40
developmental milestones, children's
language 43-65
diachronic studies 38
dialects 27-8, 152, 154-8
dictionaries 33-4
disabled and language 126, 143
Dryden, John 36
Dubois and Crouch 94
dysphemisms 140

E

Early Modern English 16-17, 29-32
education 29

egocentrism 82
elicited imitation 53
Elton, Ben 126-7, 156
Elyot, Thomas 31
emotive language 138
English, origins of 13-32
Estuary English 156-8
etymologies 118
euphemisms 90, 139, 140-4
expletives 89, 93
eye witness testimony 133

F

facilitative tags 94
Fishman, Pamela 94, 96
Fletcher, P. 64
foreign words in English 176
fricatives 60, 182
Frisians, The 15

G

generative grammar 135
generative linguistics 40
genetic classification 13, 37
Global Standard English 147-9, 191
glottal stops 156, 184
grammar
            and caretaker language 77-8
            changes in 178-81
            children's use of 50, 51-5
            and dialects 155
            and Estuary English 156
            and Middle English 25
            and Old English 19
            and Old Norse 21
            and prescriptivism 34-6
            and Standard American English 149
            women's use of 89, 94-6

H

hedges, conversational 96, 102
heuristic acquisition of language 73
historical linguistics 37
Holmes, Janet 94, 98
holophrastic stage 47
Homo Habilis 6
Homo Sapiens 7-8, 10
hypercorrect grammar 96
hypertexts 189

I

idiolects 147
imaginative use of language 73
'imitation and reinforcement'
    theory 66-8, 69-74
'inkhorn' terms 32
instrumental use of language 72
intensifiers, sexual differences
    of use 89, 95
interactional use of language 72
Internet 'conversations' 190
intonation 62-3, 90, 93

J

jargon 168
Jesperson, Otto 87
Johnson, Dr Samuel 33-4
jokes 90
Jones, Sir William 37
Jutes, The 15

K

Keith, Lois 124
King James Bible 32
Komarovsky, Mira 91
Kramer, Cheris 93

L

Labov, William 160, 161, 166-7
Lakoff, Robin 88-90, 96, 98,
99, 100, 143
Language Acquisition Device 84
language
            accommodation in 166-7
            and age variation 159
            changes in 169-85
            and class variations 161-7
            and ethnic variations 160
            functions of 71
            global spread of 11-12
            origins of 2-8
            phonological function of 71
            and prejudice 121-5
            universalist view of 135
larynx 9
Latin 19, 36
legislation and language bias 114
Lenneburg, Eric 69
lexical changes 172-7
linguistic determinism 130
linguistics 37-41

Loftus, Elizabeth 133
'logical mistakes' in language 69
Lowth, Bishop Robert 35, 180
Luchsinger and Arnold 93

M

McNeill, D. 71
Mairs, Nancy 143-4
melodic utterance stage 46
men and covert prestige 164-5
mental grammar 4, 40
metaphors 138
Middle English 16-17, 23-8
minimal responses 104
modal tags 94
Modern English 16-17, 32
monogenesis 12

N

natural selection 10
Neanderthals 7, 9
neatening, principle of 178, 181
negative politeness 97-8
negatives, use of 55, 138, 156
Nelson, Katherine 71
Neogrammarians 37, 39
neologisms 172-4, 177
neutral pronoun replacement 126, 128
nonce words 174
Normans, The 22

O

O'Barr and Atkins
O'Donoghue, Denise 100
Old English 16-17, 18-22, 37
Old Norse 21
onomatopoeia 138
Operant Conditioning theory 66-8, 69-74, 80
oratory 137-8
overt prestige 164-5

P

parcipitative reading 189
performative use of language 74
personal use of language 73
pharyngeal cavities 10
Philips, J.R. 77
phonology 44-5
    and caretaker language 75
    and children 44, 45, 50, 59-63
    and sex variations 93

and women 90
Piaget, Jean 82-4
Pinker, Steven 6
politeness 90, 97-100
politically correct language (PC) 123, 125
polygenesis 11
positive politeness 97-8
power in language
    commercial language 139
    dysphemisms 140
    euphemisms 140-4
    eyewitness testimony 133-4
    oratory 137-9
    Sapir-Whorf hypothesis 130-2
Universalism 135-6
pragmatics
    and caretaker language 78-9
    and children 44, 45, 50, 64-5
prejudice and language 121-5
prescriptive grammars 35, 39
prescriptivism 34-6
prestigious variants 161-3
Primitive Germanic 15
printing 29
pronunciation 156, 182-5
Proto-Indo-European language 13
proto-language 5
psycholinguistic model 82-4

Q

qualifiers, sexual differences in usage 95
questions
    and children 54
    rhetorical 138
    sexual variations in 94-5
    tag 89, 94-5, 102, 156
    and women 89

R

racism and language 115-20
Received Pronunciation (RP) 148,
152-3, 154
reduplication 61
regional variations 151-8
regulatory use of language 72
repetiton in oratory 138
representational use of language 74
rhetorical questions 138
Richelieu, Cardinal 36

S

St Augustine 18, 19
Sapir-Whorf hypothesis 130-2, 132-4
Saussure, Ferdinand De 38-40
Saxons, The 15
semantic rule and sexism 128
semantics
    and caretaker language 76
    and children 50, 56-8
seriation 83
sexism in language 106-14, 128
Shakespeare, William 32
silences, conversational 104
similes 138
Skinner, B. F. 66-8, 69-74, 79, 80
slang words 159
social class and language 161-7
sound changes 182-5
speech development 9-10
spelling 23, 31, 149
Spender, Dale 95, 128, 103
Standard American English (SAE) 149, 160
Standard English 25-8, 148-9, 155
Swift, Jonathan 36
synchronic studies 38
Slobin and Welsh 53

T

tag questions 89, 94-5, 102, 156
telegraphic stage milestone 49
thought versus language debate 129-36
Trudgill 162-4
two word stage milestone 48

U

Universalism 40, 135

V

velar sounds 60
verb tenses 130
Vikings, The 20-1
vocabulary
    children's 56-8
    comprehension 57-8
    and dialect 155
    Early Modern English 30-2
    Middle English 24
    neologisms and 172-4, 177
    new 187-8
variations in 149

women's 89, 91

W

Weir, Ruth 83
West, Candace 100
West, E. G. 105
William the Conqueror 22
women and prestige language 164, 165

Woods, Nicola 100
Woolf, Virginia 112
word meanings 175, 177
work words, women's 89, 91

Zimmerman and West 103-4

GENERAL

Bolinger, Dwight and Sears, Donald A. ASPECTS OF LANGUAGE 3RD ED
    Harcourt Bruce and Jovanovich Inc 1981
Bolinger, Dwight LANGUAGE THE LOADED WEAPON Longman 1980
Bryson, Bill THE MOTHER TONGUE Penguin 1990
Crystal, David THE CAMBRIDGE ENCYCLOPEDIA OF LANGUAGE.
    Cambridge University Press 1987
Crystal, David THE CAMBRIDGE ENCYCLOPEDIA OF THE ENGLISH LANGUAGE
    Cambridge University Press 1995
Montgomery, Martin AN INTRODUCTION TO LANGUAGE AND SOCIETY
    Routledge 1988
Pinker, Steven THE LANGUAGE INSTINCT THE NEW SCIENCE OF LANGUAGE AND MIND
    Allan Lane, The Penguin Press 1994

HISTORY

Aitchison, Jean LINGUISTICS Hodder and Stoughton 1978
Wilson E.O. ANIMAL COMMUNICATION Scientific American, September1972
J.L Gould and Marler P. LEARNING BY INSTINCT, Scientific American 1987
Baugh, Albert C. and Cable, Thomas A HISTORY OF THE ENGLISH LANGUAGE
    3RD ED. Routledge 1978
Bolton, W. F. and Crystal, David (Ed.) THE ENGLISH LANGUAGE
    (the Penguin History of Literature Series) Penguin 1993
Jean, Georges WRITING, THE STORY OF ALPHABETS AND SCRIPTS
    Thames and Hudson 1992
Lambert, David THE CAMBRIDGE GUIDE TO PREHISTORIC MAN Cambridge 1987
Potter, Simeon OUR LANGUAGE Penguin 1976
Strang, Barbara M. H. A HISTORY OF ENGLISH Methuen 1970
Wakelyn, Martyn THE ARCHEOLOGY OF ENGLISH Batsford 1980
Gordon, W. Terrence SAUSSURE FOR BEGINNERS 1996 Writers and Readers Ltd

CHILD LANGUAGE ACQUISITION

Aitchison, Jean THE ARTICULATE MAMMAL AN INTRODUCTION TO PSYCHOLINGUISTICS
Routledge 1989

Beattie, Geoffrey and Ellis, Andrew THE PSYCHOLOGY OF LANGUAGE AND
COMMUNICATION Lawrence Erlbaum Assoc. Ltd 1988

Berko, J. and Brown, R. PSYCHOLINGUISTIC RESEARCH METHODS IN P.H. MUSSEN
ED. HANDBOOK OF RESEARCH METHODS IN CHILD DEVELOPMENT
Wiley, 1960

Brown, Roger Cazden, C. and Bellugi, U. THE CHILD'S GRAMMAR FROM I TO III.
IN HILL, J.P. (ED) MINNESOTA SYMPOSIUM ON CHILD PSYCHOLOGY VOL. II
PG. 70 -71 University of Minnesota Press, 1969

Blake, N. F. and Moorhead, Jean INTRODUCTION TO THE ENGLISH LANGUAGE
MacMillan 1993

Clark , R., Hutchison S. and Van Buren P. COMPREHENSION AND PRODUCTION IN
LANGUAGE ACQUISITION 1974 #10, pg 46

Cruttenden, Alan AN EXPERIMENET INVOLVING COMPREHENSION OF INTONATION
IN CHILDREN FROM SEVEN TO TEN JOURNAL OF CHILD LANGUAGE, 1974 #1
221 - 231

Crystal, David LISTEN TO YOUR CHILD Penguin 1986

Dale, Phillip S. LANGUAGE DEVELOPMENT STRUCTURE AND FUNCTION Holt
Rinehart and Winston 1976

Gleitman, Lila, R. and Wanner, Eric (Eds.) LANGUAGE ACQUISITION: THE STATE
OF THE ART Cambridge University Press 1982

McTear, Michael CHILDREN'S CONVERSATION Blackwell 1985

Nelson, K. STRUCTURE AND STRATEGY IN LEARNING TO TALK. Monographs of the
Society of Research for Child Development #149 pg 38 1973

Opie, Iona and Peter, THE LORE AND LANGUAGE OF SCHOOL CHILDREN Oxford
University Press 1997

Phillips, J.R. 'SYNTAX AND VOCABULARY OF MOTHERS' SPEECH TO YOUNG
CHILDREN: AGE AND SEX COMPARISONS.' Child Development #44, 1973 pg.
182 - 185 (Quoted in Phillip S. Dale 1976 pg. 142)

Slobin, D.I., and Welsh, C.A. 'ELICITED IMITATION AS A RESEARCH TOOL IN
DEVELOPMENTAL PSYCHOLINGUISTICS' (1967) in **Ferguson and Slobin** (1973)
quoted in Aitchison, 1989 pg. 159

Snow, C.E. 'The development of conversation between mothers and babies' Journal of Child Language # 4, pg.1-22 1977 Quoted in McTear 1985

Wang, William, S. Y.(Ed.) THE EMERGEANCE OF LANGUAGE DEVELOPMENT AND EVOLUTION W. H. Freeman and co. 1991

Weir, R. LANGUAGE IN THE CRIB THE HAGUE: Mouton, 1962 (Phillip S. Dale, Language Development, Structure and Function pg. 153)

LANGUAGE, SEX AND POWER

Andersen, Roger THE POWER AND THE WORD Paladin 1988

Atkinson, Max OUR MASTERS VOICES Methuen: London 1984 (quoted in Andersen 1988)

Beard, Henry and Cerf, Christopher THE OFFICIAL POLITICALLY CORRECT DICTIONARY AND HANDBOOK Grafton, Harper Collins 1992

Brend, Ruth 'MALE-FEMALE INTONATION PATTERNS IN AMERICAN ENGLISH' p.84 - 87 OF LANGUAGE AND SEX: DIFFERENCE AND DOMINANCE (ED. BARRIE THORNE AND NANCY HENLEY) Newbury House, Rowley, Mass. 1975 (quoted in Spender 1980)

Brown, Penelope and Leivson, Stephen POLITENESS: SOME UNIVERSALS IN LANGUAGE USAGE Cambridge University Press 1987 (quoted in Holmes 1995)

Cameron, Deborah and Coates, Jennifer (Eds.) WOMEN IN THEIR SPEECH COMMUNITIES Longman 1989

Carmichael, L. et al AN EXPERIMENTAL STUDY OF THE EFFECT OF LANGUAGE ON THE REPRESENTATION OF VISUALLY PERCEIVED FORM Journal of Experimental Psychology p73-86 of # 15, 1932 (quoted in Gross 1992)

Coates, Jennifer WOMEN, MEN AND LANGUAGE Longman 1993

Dubois, Betty Lou and Crouch, Isabel 'THE QUESTION OF TAG QUESTIONS IN WOMEN'S SPEECH: THEY DON'T REALLY USE MORE OF THEM DO THEY?' p.289 - 294 of Language in Society #4 1975 quoted in Spender 1980

Fishman, Pamela 'CONVERSATIONAL INSECURITY' p.127-132 of LANGUAGE: SOCIAL PSYCHOLOGICAL PERSPECTIVES (Eds: Giles, Howard, Robinson, W. Peter, and Smith, Phillip M.) Pergamon Press, Oxford 1980(a) quoted in Coates 1993

Gross, Richard D. PSYCHOLOGY THE SCIENCE OF MIND AND BEHAVIOUR Hodder and Staughton 1993

Hall, Linda 'LANGUAGE, RACE AND COLOUR' (Ch. 7 of ANTI RACISM AN ASSAULT ON EDUCATION AND VALUE Ed. Frank Palmer) The Sherwood Press 1986

Holmes, Janet WOMEN, MEN AND POLITENESS Longman 1995

Holmes, Janet 'HEDGING YOUR BETS AND SITTING ON THE FENCE: SOME EVIDENCE FOR HEDGES AS SUPPORT STRUCTURES' Te Reo 27 p47-62 1984 (quoted in Cameron and Coates 1989)

Howard, Phillip NEW WORDS FOR OLD Hamish Hamilton Ltd. 1977

Howe, Florence and Saxton, Masha (Eds.) WITH WINGS: AN ANTHOLOGY OF LITERATURE BY WOMEN WITH DISABILITIES Virago 1988

Jespersen, Otto LANGUAGE, ITS NATURE, DEVELOPMENT AND ORIGIN George Allen and Unwin, London 1922 quoted in Spender 1982

Justman, Stewart THE JEWISH HOLOCAUST FOR BEGINNERS Writers and Readers 1995

Keith, Lois (Ed.) MUSTN'T GRUMBLE: WRITING BY DISABLE WOMEN The Women's Press 1994

Komarovsky, Mira BLUE COLLAR MARRIAGE Random House 1962 (quoted in Andersen 1988)

Kramer, Cheris FOLK LINGUISTICS Psychology Today 8: 82 - 85 1974 (quoted in Coates 1993)

Kramer, Cheris STEREOTYPES OF WOMEN'S SPEECH: THE WORDS FROM CARTOONS Journal of Popular Culture 8(3): 624 - 38 (quoted in Coates 1993)

Lakoff, Robin LANGUAGE: A WOMAN'S PLACE Harper Rowe 1975

Loftus, E.F and Palmer, J.C RECONSTRUCTION OF AUTOMOBILE DESTRUCTION: AN EXAMPLE OF THE INTERACTION BETWEEN LANGUAGE AND MEMORY The Journal of Verbal Learning and Verbal Behaviour p. 585-589 of #13, 1974

Luchsinger, R. and Arnold, G.E. VOICE SPEECH AND LANGUAGE! Constable 1965 quoted in Spender 1980

Mattingly, Ignatius 'SPEAKER VARIATION AND VOCAL TRACT SIZE' The Journal of the Acoustical Society of America vol. 39 p. 1219, 1966/1969(?) quoted in Andersen 1988

Mills, Jane WOMAN WORDS Virago 1991

O'Barr, William and Atkins, Bowman K. "WOMEN'S LANGUAGE' or 'POWERLESS LANGUAGE'?' p.93-110 of WOMEN AND LANGUAGE IN LITERATURE AND SOCIETY (Eds: McConnell-Ginet et al.) Praeger, New York 1980 quoted in Coates 1993

Spender, Dale MAN MADE LANGUGE Routledge and Keegan Paul 1980

Stanley, Julia P.'THE SEXIST TRADITION: WORDS AND MEANING' 2.5 - 10 p. 8 of # 27 Iowa English Bulletin 1978 (quoted in Spender 1980)

Stanley, Julia PARADIGMATIC WOMAN; THE PROSTITUTE Linguistic Society of

America 1973 (quoted in Spender 1980)

West, Candace 'NOT JUST 'DOCTOR'S ORDERS' DIRECTIVE-RESPONSE SEQUENCES IN PATIENT'S VISITS TO WOMEN AND MEN PHYSICIANS' from p.85-112 of Discourse and Society #1 part1 1990 (quoted in Coates 1993)

West, Candace 'WHEN THE DOCTOR IS A 'LADY': POWER, STATUS AND GENDER IN PHYSICIAN-PATIENT ENCOUNTERS' from p.87-106 of Symbolic Interaction # 7 1984 (a) quoted in Coates 1993

West, Candace 'ROUTINE COMPLICATIONS: TROUBLES WITH TALK BETWEEN DOCTORS AND PATIENTS' Indiana University Press 1984 (b) quoted in Coates 1993

Woods, Nicola 'TALKING SHOP: SEX AND STATUS AS DETERMINANTS OF FLOOR APPORTIONMENT IN A WORK SETTING' Ch.10 of Cameron and Coates 1989

Woolf, Virginia 'WOMEN AND FICTION' (from Collected Essays: Virginia Woolf Vol. 2, Ed. Leonard Woolf) Chatto and Windus 1972 quoted in Spender 1980

Zimmerman, Don and West, Candace 'SEX ROLES, INTERRUPTIONS AND SILENCES IN CONVERSATION' FROM P.105-129 OF LANGUAGE AND SEX: DIFFERENCE AND DOMINANCE (Eds: Thorne, B. and Henley, N.) Newbury House, Rowley Massachusetts 1975

LANGUAGE CHANGE

Aitchison, Jean LANGUAGE CHANGE: PROGRESS OR DECAY? 2ND EDITION Cambridge University Press 1991

Bauer, Laurie WATCHING ENGLISH CHANGE Longman 1994

Burchfield , Robert THE ENGLISH LANGUAGE Oxford University Press 1985

Burchfield, Robert UNLOCKING THE LANGUAGE Faber and Faber Ltd. 1989

Cameron, Deborah VERBAL HYGIENE Routledge 1995

Coggle, Paul DO YOU SPEAK ESTUARY? Bloomsbury publishing ltd. 1993

Fromkin, Victoria and Rodman, Robert AN INTRODUCTION TO LANGUAGE (4TH ED.) Holt, Rinehart and Winston 1988

Goodman, Sharon and Graddol, David (eds) REDESIGNING ENGLISH: NEW TEXTS NEW IDENTITIES Routledge 1996

Holmes, Janet AN INTRODUCTION TO SOCIOLINGUISTICS Longman 1992

Honey, John DOES ACCENT MATTER? Faber and Faber Ltd. 1989

Howard, Philip THE STATE OF THE LANGUAGE Penguin 1984

Labov, William SOCIOLINGUISTIC PATTERNS Philidelphia PA: University of Pennsylvania Press 1972

McMahon, April, M.S. UNDERSTANDING LANGUAGE CHANGE Cambridge
  University Press 1994

Montgomery Martin AN INTRODUCTION TO LANGUAGE AND SOCIETY
  Methuen and co Ltd 1986

O'Donnell, W.R. and Todd Loretto VARIETY IN CONTEMPORARY ENGLISH
  Unwin Hyman Ltd 1980

Tinkel, A.J. EXPLORATIONS IN LANGUAGE Cambridge University Press 1988

Trudgill, Peter THE DIALECTS OF ENGLAND Blackwell publishers 1990

Trudgill, Peter THE SOCIAL DIFFERENCIATION OF ENGLISH IN NORWICH
  Cambridge University Press 1972

Man Made Language by Dale Spender, London, 1982 by permission of River Oram Press.

An introduction of Language and Society by Martin Montgomery, London 1986 reprinted by permission of Methuen & Co.

Women, Man and Politeness by Holmes., reprinted by permission of Addison Wesley Longman Ltd.

Women in their Speech Communities by Coates/Cameroon, reprinted by permission of Addison Wesley Longman Ltd.

On Being a Cripple by Nancy Mars from *With Wings: An Anthology of Literature by Women with Disabilities,* ed. By Marsha Saxton and Florence Howe, published by the Feminist Press and with permission of Bobbe Seigel Literary Agency.

Gridlock, by Ben Elton, reprinted by permission of Little Brown & Co (YK)

Smashing the Glass Ceiling, by Henry Porter **The Guardian,** May 26, 1997. Reprinted by permission.

November 21, 1993, reprinted from the **Washington Times**

New Words For Old by Philip Howard reprinted by permission of Penguin Books (UK) Ltd.

PC World - May 1997 pg. 103 by Philipa Spanner, reprinted by permission of PC World.

Language and Women's Place by Robin Lakoff reprinted by permission of Harper Collins Publishers Inc.

(author's by line and name of author 1979, Los Angeles times. Reprinted by permission